# ENTERING BASIC

JOHN R. SACK
Amdahl Corporation
Sunnyvale, California


JUDITH L. MEADOWS
University of California
Berkeley

SCIENCE RESEARCH ASSOCIATES, INC.
Chicago, Palo Alto, Toronto,
Henley-on-Thames, Sydney

A Subsidiary of IBM

Illustrations on pages 12, 13, 14, are reprinted and adapted with permission from INFORMATION PROCESSING, by Marilyn Bohl. © 1971, Science Research Associates, Inc.

Problem 6 on page 56 and problem 3 on page 64 are reprinted with permission from INTRODUCTION TO COMPUTER SCIENCE by C. W. Gear. © 1973, Science Research Associates, Inc.

To Lynne and Oliver

The main objective of this book is to teach you to solve data-processing problems using BASIC, a programming language developed at Dartmouth College by John Kemeny and Thomas Kurtz. The book also provides the newcomer to computer science with an overview of the computer and its operations. The first two chapters are intended solely as an introduction to the computer and to interactive processing. If you are already comfortable with these fundamental concepts and terminology, you can skip to the discussion of BASIC that begins in chapter 3.

Programming in BASIC, a straightforward algebraic language, will help you understand the fundamental concepts of computer processing. At the same time, BASIC is an ideal first step toward more complicated programming languages such as FORTRAN, COBOL, and ALGOL. Like the Roman god Janus who faces both ways, BASIC faces the needs of those just entering the world of automated data processing as well as those departing for its more stratified plateaus.

Finally, this book can be used to complement C. W. Gear's *Introduction to Computer Science* (Science Research Associates, 1973). Some of the problem material developed here is extracted from Gear's text. In addition, his book is frequently referred to for detailed discussions of specific points that go beyond the scope of this work. The two books are, however, mutually independent.

While many people have been instrumental in assembling and preparing this material, we wish particularly to acknowledge the help of Don Cantor of the Computer Corporation of America, Marilyn Bohl (whose book *Information Processing* suggested much of the organization of our first two chapters), and the editorial staff of Science Research Associates. We also thank R.A.I.R. Inc. of Mountain View, California, for letting us use their computer and terminals.

JLM
JRS

# PREFACE

# CONTENTS

## THE ROLE OF THE COMPUTER IN PROBLEM SOLVING

*The primary function of the computer is problem solving.* Like its predecessors—the electric calculator, the slide rule, and the clerk hunched over his ledgers—the computer is simply a tool for performing data-processing tasks. It was developed as a refinement of its predecessors because the problems to be solved in our modern world have become more refined and more complex. Calculating the location of a spaceship rocketing toward the moon or generating tons of reports on the checking account activity of millions of bank customers exceeds the capabilities of a labor force using yesterday's tools.

*The primary function of the computer programmer is to provide a plan for solving a problem in a form acceptable to the machine.* This plan, in its machine-acceptable form, is called a *program*.

There are, then, two areas of operation to be considered in problem solving by computer: the computer machinery or *hardware* that performs the mechanics of the operation and the programs or *software* that direct the machine's functioning.

## COMPUTER HARDWARE

Describing the components of a computer system is like trying to describe the features and characteristics of an automobile. Obviously, the special features of a Volkswagen and a Ferrari cannot be encompassed in a single description. Even within a family of automobiles, such as the various Chevrolet models, there are significant differences in features, price, and performance. So too with computer systems.

All computer systems are in some respects alike. All can be programmed to do certain basic operations such as reading and writing data or performing mathematical calculations, just as all automobiles can be accelerated or stopped. But one computer may perform in a millionth of a second a calculation that requires a full thousandth of a second on another

Chapter

# 1

# FUNDAMENTALS of COMPUTING

machine. One may allow us to store millions of data items, while another limits us to thousands of items. One computer system may include a device for processing reels of magnetic tape, while another may include devices to read and punch cards or paper tape. Even within a family of computers, such as the IBM 360 series or the CDC 6000 series, there are significant differences in features, price, and performance.

The capabilities of a computer system can generally be distinguished by the operational speed and flexibility of its central processing unit (CPU) and by the number and types of *peripheral* devices (used for data input, output, and storage) attached to the CPU. A schematic representation of these elements also shows the three sequential steps of problem solving by computer: data input, processing of the data, and the resultant output.

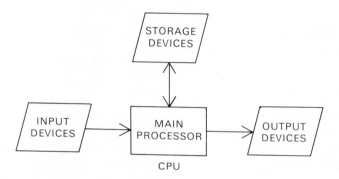

Thus a very simple payroll program might:

- Read punched cards containing employee numbers and hours worked
- Read a payroll master file containing each employee's name, number, hourly wage, year-to-date total wages received, and salary deductions
- In the CPU, match employee numbers and calculate wages and deductions for the current pay period
- Update the payroll master file with the new year-to-date totals
- On a high-speed printer, print the checks containing employee name and salary received.

### The Central Processing Unit

The relation of the CPU to the rest of a computer system is analogous to the relation of the human brain to the rest of the body. The CPU's *control section* directs the activity of the peripheral devices much as the brain directs the movements of the arms or legs.[1] The *arithmetic/logic unit* of the CPU performs the basic mathematical operations (addition, subtraction, multiplication, division) and also moves, shifts, and compares data.

Like our brain, the CPU also contains a memory unit, the *primary storage area* of the computer system. This storage holds the program instructions being executed and the data the program is processing. The control section can access the instructions and the data as required, by referencing addresses assigned to each storage location.

You could think of these storage locations as a cluster of post office boxes. Suppose Charles Nelson rents box 3000 for two months. He can ask for his mail by saying either, "Give me what's in box 3000" or "Give me the mail for Nelson." If Ed Stelmach later rents box 3000, he too can ask for his mail by either box or name. The contents of each post office box can be accessed by its fixed, *absolute* address (3000) or by a *symbolic*, *variable* name (Stelmach or Nelson). The same is true of a computer's primary storage locations, as you'll see more clearly in later chapters.

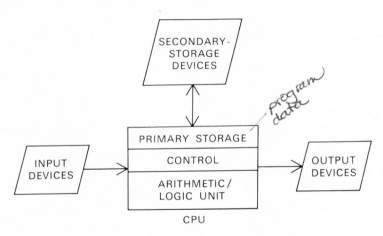

### Peripheral Devices

The entire range of input, output, and storage devices available to today's computer user can't possibly be described in this brief overview. However, the factors determining the makeup of a system will give you a feel for some of the distinctions between devices.

For example, does a particular computing center process jobs that store large volumes of data? Is printed output necessary and, if so, how much? Does the user simply require a quick answer to a single problem? Is processing speed important? What are the economic considerations?

Input devices can read data recorded as holes punched into cards or paper tape, as magnetized particles on magnetic tape or disc, or as characters on paper documents (such as the numbers at the bottom of a check); or they can accept data typed at a keyboard terminal. Card and paper-tape readers are relatively slow, but also relatively inexpensive. Data can be accessed more quickly from the more expensive magnetic recording media. Magnetic tapes, discs, drums, and data cells can also hold enormous amounts of information in a small space, providing what is often called *secondary storage* for the system.

Keyboard-terminal units such as console typewriters, teletypewriters, or visual-display devices resembling TV tubes can provide a direct link between the user and the computer while a program is running. During such *interactive* processing the primary emphasis is on rapid response. The great bulk of programming in BASIC is done interactively; this mode of communication is described in greater detail in chapter 2.

Output devices accept results from the CPU and write or save the results for human use or for input to subsequent programs or machines other than computers. They can record information on cards, paper tape, or magnetizable surfaces. They can print information or illustrations on paper, direct the same information to visual-display devices, or even state results verbally.

Output to be read by humans is usually printed. A high-speed line printer is used most often when much data is to be printed. A console typewriter suffices for simple printed messages or short reports or for low-budget systems.

Output to be read by another program may be punched into cards or paper tape. Again, punched media are processed slowly and are bulky if much data is to be recorded. They do have the advantages of low cost and of being manually correctable. Magnetic tapes, discs, drums, or data cells are the best storage media for massive amounts of data. They are compact and can be processed quickly. The stored data cannot be read or manipulated manually, however, and magnetic-coding devices are more expensive than punch units.

In summary, several points can be gleaned from this short discussion of peripheral devices.

1   A computer configuration can be tailored to the requirements of its users.

2   The faster the devices and the greater the storage capacity of the recording media, the higher the cost of the computer system.

3   Some peripheral devices (such as magnetic-tape drives) can be used for input, output, *and* storage of data; other devices (such as line printers) are limited to a single use.

4   Input to a program can come from a complex of sources (such as card, terminal, and disc); output data can likewise be distributed to several media as part of a single job.

## COMPUTER SOFTWARE

### System Software

Many computer operations are common to almost all systems. They include such tasks as monitoring the input/output flow, controlling access to the CPU if the computer system is shared by several programs, or calculating computer usage for accounting and billing purposes.

To save duplication of effort, programs or routines to perform these tasks are usually developed by computer manufacturers and delivered to customers with the hardware as part of their total computer system. These programs are called the *system software*.

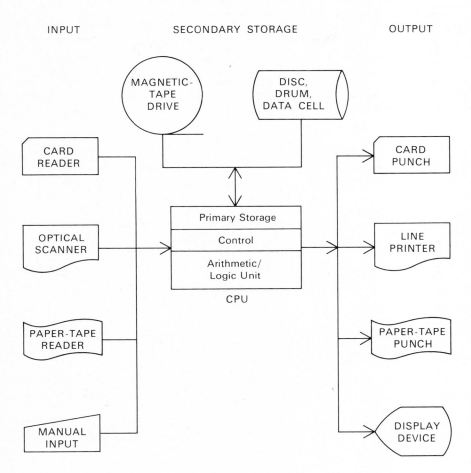

FIGURE 1–1    Peripheral Devices

Other functions, such as certain mathematical or data-sorting routines, have such general and frequent applications that they are often supplied along with the system software as a library of programs accessible to all users.

### User Software

For certain applications, general-purpose programs are inadequate. In such a case, a program must be tailored to the unique requirements of the job. The program is normally developed in four stages: initial design,[2] coding, assembly or compilation, and debugging or testing.

**Initial Design**  Before a program can be coded, its overall logic and a clear definition of the problem must be worked out—the broad design must be sketched before the details are painted in. This is done most easily with a *program flowchart*.

Entire books have been written on the subject of flowcharting,[3] but for our purposes only a few symbols need be defined.

Start or end of program

Input/Output operation

Processing

Decision

Connector

The logic of every program, in its most general form, can be summarized by the following flowchart.

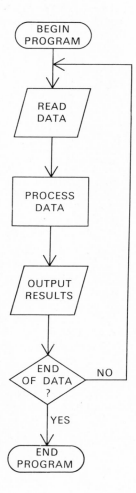

FIGURE 1–2  Summary of Program Logic

The payroll program mentioned earlier could be flowcharted very generally as follows:

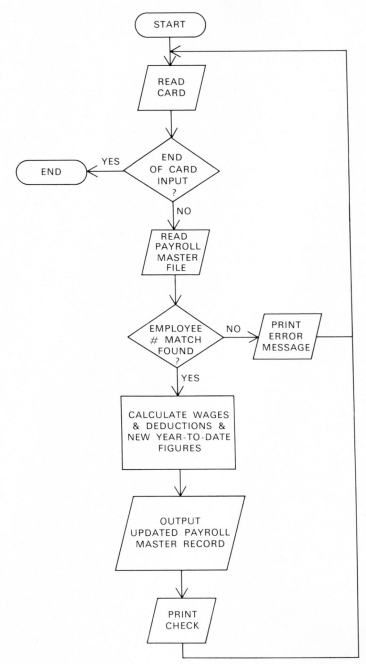

FIGURE 1–3   The Payroll Program

**Coding the Source Program**    Having sketched out an approach to the problem, coding of program instructions can begin. The form the *source program* takes will depend on the programming language selected. Programming languages, like computer configurations, are designed with particular types of jobs in mind. The COBOL language, for example, is usually chosen for business applications; algebraic languages such as BASIC and FORTRAN are more useful for scientific or mathematical applications; PL/1 is used in both business and scientific applications; assembly languages such as BAL or COMPASS are used most often in very sophisticated programming tasks such as system software development.

In noninteractive (or "batch") programming situations, the coded source program is punched into cards and the resultant *source deck* is then passed to the next stage —program assembly or compilation.

**Assembly/Compilation**    While a program in its source code form can be read easily by the programmer, it is not yet intelligible to the computer. Before it can be used, it must be translated into the machine's language. This is done either by an *assembler* program or by a *compiler*, depending on the programming language used.[4]

An assembler program translates (or *assembles*) assembly-language programs into machine language. When programming in an assembly language, one source statement must normally be coded for each machine-language instruction needed.

Compiler programs translate (or *compile*) source programs written in so-called high-level languages such as COBOL, BASIC, FORTRAN, and PL/1. Compilers are smarter than assemblers. In addition to allowing for selection of a language appropriate to the application, they often reduce coding requirements by expanding a single source statement into several machine-language instructions. A "print" statement, for example, might be expanded into machine instructions that move data to an output buffer area, cause the print device to print the data, and check for possible error conditions.

An important point to note here is that assemblers and compilers are themselves programs: they perform input, processing, and output functions. Their input is the coded source program. Their main processing function is translating the source program into an *object program* that can be executed by the computer. Their output normally consists of a listing of the source program, diagnostic notes on any errors detected in the program, and (if the program contains no serious errors) the object program. The object program may be punched into cards or paper tape or saved on some magnetic-storage device. Compilers and assemblers are supplied by the computer manufacturer as part of the library of general-purpose programs.

**Debugging/Testing**    Very few programs are completely error free the first time they are coded and punched. Some errors are flagged by the assembler or compiler program when it tries to translate the source code. However, even after these errors have been corrected (when the program is *syntactically* correct according to the rules of the language used), the program can still contain design or *logic* errors. The program may run without meeting all the requirements of its earlier problem definition. To detect these *bugs* in program logic, we must create data that represents as many as possible of the conditions the program will face, and then run this data through the program.

The entire area of program design and testing is extremely important and is discussed in more detail in chapter 12. You should refer to chapter 12 frequently when you begin programming in BASIC.

**Summary**    The stages of program development can be summarized by the following diagram.

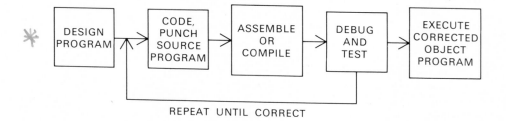

```
DESIGN      →   CODE,      →   ASSEMBLE   →   DEBUG     →   EXECUTE
PROGRAM         PUNCH          OR             AND           CORRECTED
                SOURCE         COMPILE        TEST          OBJECT
                PROGRAM                                     PROGRAM
```

REPEAT UNTIL CORRECT

**EXERCISES**

1. Describe the differences and relationships between the following pairs of terms:

> Hardware—Software
> CPU—Peripheral Devices
> Input—Output
> Primary Storage—Secondary Storage
> Absolute Address—Symbolic Address
> System Program—User Program
> Source Program—Object Program
> Assembler—Compiler
> Syntax Error—Logic Error

2. Visit a computer installation. Discuss the computer configuration with the manager of computer operations. Find out what input/output devices are available and what their speeds are. Ask what kinds of jobs are run and which programming languages are used. If possible, watch a program being compiled and/or run.

**FOOTNOTES AND REFERENCES**

1 Gear, C. W., *Introduction to Computer Science*, Science Research Associates, Chicago, 1973. See section 2.4 on computer control.

2 Initial program design is itself a multiphase operation. See chapter 12.

3 See, for example, *Flowcharting Techniques* by Marilyn Bohl, Science Research Associates, Chicago, 1971.

4 Gear, section 4.2, "Language Translators." See also his discussion of an assembler language, section 2.6.1 and 2.6.2.

## DEFINITIONS

If this is your first attempt at programming, or if you are a programmer accustomed solely to batch-processing operations, you will find interactive processing to be a different world with its own terminology and a significantly advanced approach to problem solving and programming.

The terms *online, real time, time sharing, teleprocessing,* and *conversational* are all related to interactive processing.[1] Most of them are used loosely as synonyms, which, in fact, they aren't.

*Interactive processing* refers to a direct link between the user and the computer. Seated at his terminal, the user enters his data and receives results directly—displayed on his own machine. Such immediate interaction between the user and the computer is the single greatest advantage of this mode of processing.

Using traditional batch-processing procedures, a programmer codes his program, has it punched into cards, ships the program to a central operating area where it undergoes further handling, and finally receives a printed listing of the program. If it contains errors, he must code the corrections and repeat the entire procedure. A program might require several days or weeks to debug at this rate.

In *interactive programming*, however, all intermediate handling is eliminated. The terminal user types in his program statements which are entered into the computer's storage and displayed on his terminal simultaneously. Syntax errors become evident immediately and can be corrected on the spot. After the program has been entered into the computer, it can be compiled, tested, and executed at the terminal. Thus, a procedure that formerly extended over several days or weeks is reduced to a matter of minutes or hours.

Interactive processing must be performed *online*, although online processing need not be interactive. The term online refers to a system in which all necessary devices are immediately accessible (online) to the computer. A user need only enter his input data, which is processed immediately. If the output results are

Chapter

# 2

# Interactive Processing

returned quickly enough to be useful in some current activity, a *real-time* environment has been created. Common examples of this processing situation are airline and motel reservation systems, savings account processing, and department store sales transactions in which cash registers are linked to computers. Note that in these cases the user is not a programmer, but a reservations clerk, bank teller, or sales clerk.

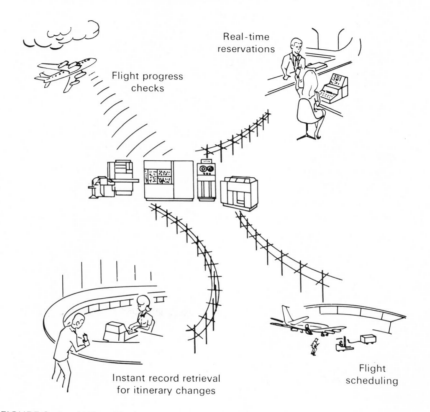

Flight progress checks

Real-time reservations

Instant record retrieval for itinerary changes

Flight scheduling

FIGURE 2–1    Airlines Real-Time Application

The most evident feature of a *time-sharing* system is, as the name implies, its ability to process several tasks simultaneously. The processing computer services one user after another, but at intervals of time measured in thousandths of a second, so each user has the illusion of commanding sole access to the system. All of the real-time examples mentioned above would probably be part of a time-sharing network. The same is true of most programming done in the BASIC language.

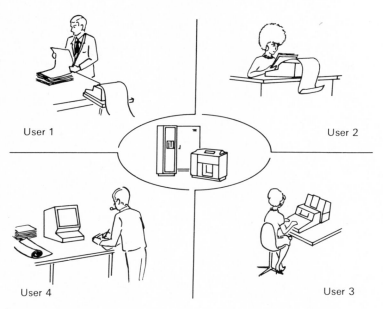

User 1

User 2

User 4

User 3

FIGURE 2–2    The Time-Sharing Cycle

In many instances the terminals used in these operations are located a considerable distance from the processing computer—scattered across a campus or town, across the country, or even around the world. Long-distance processing, called *teleprocessing*, represents a merging of two different technologies: data processing, the specialty of computer manufacturers; and communications, the specialty of AT&T and other common carriers. Data is entered at a terminal and translated by means of a communications medium (such as telephone lines, microwave-radio circuits, or electric cables) to the main processor. In interactive teleprocessing, results are transmitted immediately from the processor to the terminal.

Finally, interactive processing is sometimes called *conversational*. A conversational program or compiler responds immediately to input, telling the user if he has made an error, asking for additional information, and so on. If you are a beginner at an interactive terminal, you may find that your console exhibits all the recalcitrance of a refractory child, apparently hoping to train you before you train it (as is the wont of children). Once you do succeed in the latter, however, you will find direct communication with the computer an enjoyable and very practicable substitute for the cold uncertainty surrounding a source deck being swallowed (piecemeal, perhaps) by a remote card reader.

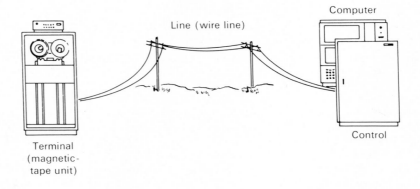

Terminal
(magnetic-
tape unit)

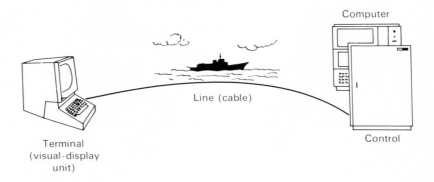

Terminal
(visual-display
unit)

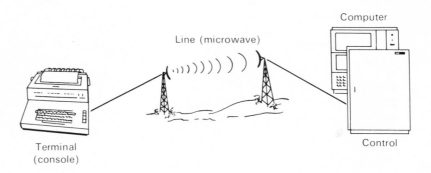

Terminal
(console)

FIGURE 2–3   Teleprocessing Systems

## TIME-SHARING SYSTEM SOFTWARE

An operational time-sharing system represents a delicate balance among an enormous complex of interacting hardware and software features. Obviously, the system must have a large storage capacity and nearly instantaneous retrieval capability to effectively manipulate the programs and/or data of its many users. As we mentioned earlier, linking the user's terminal to this processing configuration involves the interfacing of two different technologies. Supervision of this linkage is handled by the system software, a group of elaborate monitor and executive programs. These programs must handle the work demands of multiple users performing different kinds of tasks in a variety of computing languages. They must keep the entire system running efficiently in a sequence determined by priorities. If a user's job is not completed within the allotted time limit, the control routines set it aside, go on to other users' jobs, and then return to the uncompleted task. They also move data to and from storage, protect user files from other users, keep track of who is logged into the system and for how long, make corrections, and even type out preprogrammed messages to help unskilled users.

The system monitor deals primarily with the computer hardware.[2] The executive acts as the interface between the monitor and the user. It allows the user to log into and out of the system, create and manipulate files of programs or data, save and restore these files—all from his own terminal. Through the executive, a programmer can select the specific programming language (and compiler) best suited to his individual problem requirements and programming knowledge. The executive also keeps accounting records for billing and statistical purposes. It identifies the various users and keeps track of the length of time they're connected to the computer, the CPU time used, and the amount of disc storage used.

## TIME-SHARING PROGRAMMING LANGUAGES

Relatively simple programming languages are also vital in making a time-sharing system available to users with diverse backgrounds. The computer itself, as you know now, is wired to react to machine language only. A programmer must be fairly expert to handle machine language, and in any case debugging is slow. Consequently many languages have been developed that use phraseology resembling conventional English or algebraic notation. In interactive programming, the compilers that translate these languages into machine language are called directly through the system executive.

BASIC (Beginner's All-purpose Symbolic Instruction Code), the subject of this book, is an example of a simplified algebraic language.

## INTERACTIVE PROGRAMMING

The rules of a simple computer language such as BASIC can be learned fairly readily from a book, but this gives you no real feel for the language. The sooner you begin working at a terminal, the better. Hands-on learning is far quicker and more easily retained than programming rules memorized from a technical text. We've tried to keep this in mind while designing this book and hope that as you read it a terminal will be within easy reach.

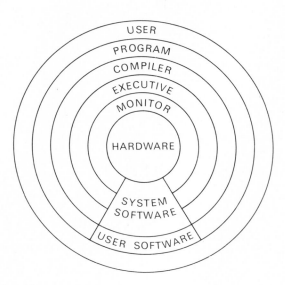

FIGURE 2—4    Interactive Programming

### BASIC and the Executive

Before you do any terminal work with BASIC, you must be able to use the executive language available at your particular installation. This simple set of commands enables you to log onto the computer system and to communicate with the executive program while you are entering, changing, or running your BASIC program. The form this language takes varies from one computing system to another and is a subject beyond the scope of this book.[3] We will, however, use some typical executive commands in our examples. The following list shows the commands used in this text and gives you an idea of the types of functions you can perform using executive commands.

SAVE      Causes a permanent copy of the current program to be stored
          on some magnetic-storage device.

UNSAVE    Deletes the permanent copy of the current program from
          storage.

LIST      Can be used to list lines, blocks of lines, or an entire program.
          LIST
          LIST 1∅,5∅—1∅∅
          LISTNH

If only the command LIST is given, as in the first example above, the current program is listed in its entirety. The second example would cause line 10 of the current program and the block of lines from 50 through 100 to be listed. LISTNH lists the program without header information (program name, date, and time of day.)

DELETE    Can be used to delete individual lines or blocks of lines, using
          the same conventions as LIST.
DELETE    1∅,7∅—12∅

Some executives include a DELETE ALL command that, like UNSAVE, deletes an entire program.

RUN    Causes the current program to be compiled and executed. RUNNH
       can be entered to run the program but suppress header informa-
       tion in the printed results.

All of the typical executive commands just described deal with the "current" program. You identify this program to the system when you log onto the computer. After you have satisfied the executive that you are a valid user and have stated that you are working in the BASIC language, the executive responds with

NEW OR OLD

or a statement to this effect. If you want to work with a program that has been entered and saved previously, type OLD and the program name. If you are creating a new program, type NEW and the program name. In either case, the named program becomes the current one.

The following diagram shows the sequence of steps followed during an interactive programming session. Note that in steps 1–3 and 5–6 you are communicating with your system's executive program. Only at step 4 do you enter instructions that become part of your BASIC program.

A sample typed program, showing BASIC statements used in conjunction with executive commands, will be given at the end of chapter 3—after we have had a first look at an actual BASIC program.

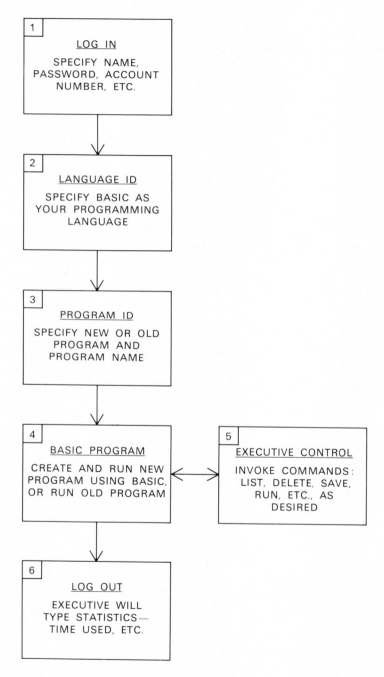

**1  LOG IN**

SPECIFY NAME,
PASSWORD, ACCOUNT
NUMBER, ETC.

**2  LANGUAGE ID**

SPECIFY BASIC AS
YOUR PROGRAMMING
LANGUAGE

**3  PROGRAM ID**

SPECIFY NEW OR OLD
PROGRAM AND
PROGRAM NAME

**4  BASIC PROGRAM**

CREATE AND RUN NEW
PROGRAM USING BASIC,
OR RUN OLD PROGRAM

**5  EXECUTIVE CONTROL**

INVOKE COMMANDS:
LIST, DELETE, SAVE,
RUN, ETC., AS
DESIRED

**6  LOG OUT**

EXECUTIVE WILL
TYPE STATISTICS—
TIME USED, ETC.

FIGURE 2–5   Sequential Steps in Interactive Programming

## Text Conventions

Whenever you program at your computer terminal you are involved in a dialogue with the system software of your installation (the executive program and the BASIC compiler). The examples in this book show both the statements you enter and the responses typed from the computer. To ensure clarity, computer output is underlined.

At the end of every executive command or program statement, you must press a special control key on your terminal (typically the carriage-return key). Since this control key usually does not print at your terminal, we will not show it in our program examples.

Zeros are slashed (∅) to avoid confusion with the letter O.

## EXERCISES

1.  The main purpose of this chapter is to introduce the terminology relating to interactive processing. To apply your newly learned wisdom, the next time you hear people talking computer jargon, casually drop the following:

    "The other day I was communicating via teleprocessing lines with our time-sharing system in _____. I logged on with the system executive, _____, entered my program, and compiled it using the BASIC compiler, which is online to our _____ computer. I easily corrected a few syntax errors and had my results in less than an hour. Interactive processing is great!"

    To fill in the blanks, find out where your computer system is located, the name of your executive, and the type and model of your computer. Study the terms to be sure you understand them. This understanding isn't really necessary to write programs in BASIC, but your friends will be impressed.

2.  Get a writeup of the executive commands and log-in procedure used by your system. You will use them in the next chapter when you start entering programs.

3.  Watch someone working at a computer terminal. Is the system conversational? (Does the system ask him questions and respond to his input?) Are there sometimes short delays before the system responds? This can happen on some time-sharing systems when many users are logged onto the system simultaneously.

## FOOTNOTES AND REFERENCES

1   An excellent discussion of these concepts can be found in *Information Processing* by Marilyn Bohl, chapter 16 (Science Research Associates, Chicago, 1971).
2   Gear, section 4.3, "Monitor."
3   The executive language discussed here is similar to what Gear calls a "job control interpreter." See his section 4.1.

## ELEMENTS OF A BASIC PROGRAM

As an introduction to programming in BASIC, consider a short program, SQUART,[1] used to print out the square roots of the numbers one through five followed by the message FINISHED. The logic for solving this problem is shown in the flowchart on the next page.

At the bottom of this page is a listing of a BASIC source program coded from this flowchart.

### Statement Numbering and Length

Our sample program consists of seven statements, each beginning with a sequence number. Sequence numbers are needed to indicate the order of statement execution.

Sequence numbers should be limited to the range 0–99999. A good programming habit is to choose numbers that allow plenty of room for later insertions. The numbering in the SQUART program, for example, permits the insertion of up to nine additional statements between statements 10 and 20.

The sequence numbers in the example are followed by blanks, but this is not a requirement. The use of blanks in BASIC is optional; their primary function is to improve program readability. Statement 50, for example, could have been entered as 5Ø IF A < 6 THEN 3Ø.

Chapter

# 3

# Introduction to BASIC

```
1Ø REM SQUARE ROOT CALCULATION
2Ø LET A=1
3Ø PRINT "THE SQUARE ROOT OF" A "IS" SQR(A)
4Ø LET A=A+1
5Ø IF A<6 THEN 3Ø
6Ø PRINT "FINISHED"
7Ø END
```

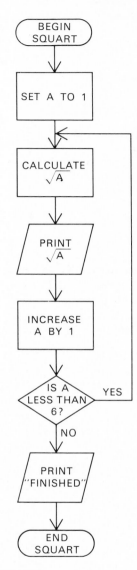

FIGURE 3–1 The Logic of SQUART

Since program statements (and data) are terminated by a carriage return, the statement length is limited to the length of the terminal carriage (usually in the range of 70–120 characters).

**Constants and Variables**[2]

**Constants** Constants are the *fixed* values used in your BASIC program. BASIC allows three kinds of constants: numerical, string, and internal.

The initial value of A (1 in statement 20 of the sample program), the incremental value (1 in statement 40), and the terminal value (6 in statement 50) are all *numerical constants*. The largest numerical constant permitted in most BASIC systems is about 5 times $10^{76}$; the smallest numerical constant is about 4 times $10^{-78}$.

BASIC accepts and displays real numbers in three formats:[3]

| | |
|---|---|
| Integer | 1, 123, 999999 |
| Decimal | 6.7, 10.0027 |
| Exponential | 4.06E8 $(4.06 \times 10^8)$ |
| | 7.2E−12 $(7.2 \times 10^{-12})$ |

When displaying numbers, BASIC selects the number format on the following basis:

1  Integer form is chosen if the number has less than seven digits and has no fraction part.

2  Decimal form is selected if the number has a fraction part and has less than seven total significant digits. (Significant digits contribute to the accuracy of the number. Leading zeros to the left of a decimal point—0023.1— and trailing zeros to the right—1.020300—are not significant digits.)

3  Exponential form is used for all other numbers.

In the last two instances, leading and trailing zeros are not shown in the printout.

*String constants* are strings of letters (A–Z), numbers (0–9), and/or special characters (such as commas and periods). In statements 30 and 60 of our example "THE SQUARE ROOT OF," "IS," and "FINISHED" are all string constants. String constants are always enclosed in quotation marks.

*Internal constants* are a special set of frequently used predefined values. The constants included in this set vary from system to system but a typical internal constant is PI that has the standard value $\pi$ or 3.14159 . . . .

**Variables**   A variable is a field whose value may change during the execution of the program. One variable (A) is used in the SQUART program. *A* is initially set to 1, later incremented to 2, and so forth.

A variable is always named by the programmer and can be a *numerical variable* (containing numerical data) or a *string variable* (containing string data) depending on the name assigned to it.

Simple numerical variables are named using any letter (A–Z) or any letter followed by a single digit (0–9).

| | |
|---|---|
| Legal: | Z |
| | B2 |

| | |
|---|---|
| Illegal: | 1A (letter must be first) |
| | AB (two letters illegal) |
| | M16 (too many characters) |
| | 22 (two digits illegal) |
| | F# (# not allowed) |

The name of a string variable is a single letter followed by a dollar sign.

Legal : A$
        B$
        Z$

Illegal : 1$ (first character must be a letter)
          $A (letter must precede $)
          AB$ (too many letters)

Many BASIC systems allow a digit as the second character of a string-variable name just as they do with simple numerical variables (for example, A1$, Z9$). The shorter form restriction is still widespread, however, and should be observed if you are unsure of the capabilities of your particular system.

String manipulation is an important feature of BASIC and is discussed in detail in chapter 10.

**A General Comment on Constants and Variables** Beginning programmers are often confused by the terms *variable name, variable value,* and *constant.* Variable values and constants are the actual data manipulated by your program when it is executed. Variable names are provided simply for your convenience to allow you to label and refer to a CPU storage location whose value may be changing while your program executes.

The following data is in computer memory when SQUART is compiled and ready to execute :

Memory | 1 | T | H | E | | S | Q | U | A | R | E | | R | O | O | T | | O | F | I | S | 1 | 6 | F | I | N | I | S | H | E | D |

Label   A                              constants   (unlabeled)

After instruction 20 (LET A = 1) is executed, the area named A will contain a 1. The rest of the areas will be unchanged. After instruction 40 (LET A = A + 1) is first executed, the area named A will contain a 2. It is incremented by 1 each time instruction 40 is executed thereafter.

Constants may be given names and used in the same way as variables even though they don't change. The following program functions identically to the SQUART program.

```
1Ø REM EXAMPLE TO CLARIFY USE OF VARIABLES AND CONSTANTS
15 LET B=1
2Ø LET A=B
23 LET X$="THE SQUARE ROOT OF"
26 LET Y$="IS"
3Ø PRINT X$; A; Y$; SQR(A)
4Ø LET A=A+B
45 LET C=6
5Ø IF A<C THEN 3Ø
55 LET Z$="FINISHED"
6Ø PRINT Z$
7Ø END
```

In this example all constants are named. (They are treated as variables.) This example is longer and more difficult to read than SQUART. There is, therefore, no advantage in naming the constants. In some programs, however, when a long constant is used many times, coding may be simplified by giving the constant a name and referring to it by that name.

### Arithmetic and Relational Operators

When we refer to *arithmetic operators* in BASIC, we mean the symbols $+$, $-$, $*$, $/$, and $\uparrow$ that are discussed in detail in chapter 4.

The *relational operators* are $=$, $<$, $>$, $<=$, $>=$, and $<>$. They are described in chapter 6.

One word of caution: the equal sign ($=$) is not always used in the same sense in BASIC as it is in ordinary mathematics. Here its meaning is often "replaced by" rather than "equals"; the $A = A + 1$ in line 40 is a valid statement in BASIC. It means "replace A with the value of $A + 1$."

### Comment Statements

The first statement in the example program, statement 10, is a REM (remark or comment) statement. It simply annotates the program, in this case explaining what the program output will be. REMs can be extremely useful for clarifying complicated programs. They can be scattered throughout a program and have no effect on its execution. Since they perform no actual processing operations, they need not be represented on a program flowchart.

### Program-Processing Operations

The actual work of program SQUART is done by the six executable statements, 20 through 70. The BASIC language elements illustrated by these statements can be divided into three categories: value assignment, input/output, and program control.

The LET statements (20 and 40) are used to assign values to variables. *Value assignment* is discussed in chapter 4.

PRINT (statements 30 and 60) is only one of several *input/output* statements. Input statements can also be used to assign values to variables indirectly. Input/output is described in chapter 5.

*Program-control* statements, represented in the sample program by the IF—THEN (50) and END (70) statements, are described in chapter 6. They include the programming concepts of branch instructions, loops, and program termination.

### Functions

Before printing the sample program output, statement 30 calculates the square root of A using SQR, one of many predefined functions supplied with BASIC. A listing of these functions and rules for defining your own functions are presented in chapter 7. The description of BASIC functions also leads to a discussion of BASIC capabilities for handling subroutines and more complicated mathematical problems (chapters 8—9).

## A SAMPLE PROGRAM RUN

The following example shows how our sample program, SQUART, might have been created. In addition to BASIC statements and executive commands, you will note the use of some teletypewriter controls (such as hitting ← to delete a character and S to stop typing).

Executive commands can be distinguished easily from BASIC statements on the console log sheet. Executive commands are not numbered. They are also distinguishable during the actual console session in that they are executed as soon as they are entered. BASIC statements are not executed until the entire program is completed and an executive command such as RUN is entered.

On the left is a record of the dialogue between programmer and computer, on the right a brief explanation of the exchange. Information printed by the system is underlined.

| | |
|---|---|
| <u>OLD OR NEW:</u>NEW:SQUART | Identify new program as SQUART. |
| <u>READY</u> | |
| 1Ø REM SQUARE ROOT CALCULATION | Begin typing program. |
| 2Ø LET A=2 | Mistake ("A" should equal 1). |
| 3Ø PRINT "THE SQUARE ROOT OF" A "IS" SQR(A) | |
| 4Ø LET A=A+1 | |
| 5Ø IF A<6 THEN 2Ø←←3Ø | Backspacing twice (←←) deletes "20." |
| LIST 5Ø | Make sure correction worked. |
| <u>5Ø IF A<6 THEN 3Ø</u> | |
| <u>READY</u> | |
| 6Ø PRINT "FINISHED" | Finish program. |
| 7Ø END | |
| <u>READY</u> | |
| LISTNH | Program is listed (without a heading). |

```
1Ø REM SQUARE ROOT CALCULATION
2Ø LET A=2
3Ø PRINT "THE SQUARE ROOT OF"A"IS"SQR(A)
4Ø LET A=A+1
5Ø IF A<6 THEN 3Ø
6Ø PRINT "FINISHED"
7Ø END
RUNNH
```
Execute program (without a heading).

```
THE SQUARE ROOT OF 2      IS 1.41421
THE SQUARE ROOT OF 3      IS 1.732Ø5
THE SQUAR
S
```
We missed SQR(1).

Hit "S" to stop printing.

```
RUNNING TIME:  ØØ.7 SECS.
2Ø LET A=1
```
Correct line 20 and try again

```
RUNNH
```

```
THE SQUARE ROOT OF 1      IS 1
THE SQUARE ROOT OF 2      IS 1.41421
THE SQUARE ROOT OF 3      IS 1.732Ø5
THE SQUARE ROOT OF 4      IS 2
THE SQUARE ROOT OF 5      IS 2.236Ø7
FINISHED
```
Now the program works as desired.

```
DONE

RUNNING TIME:  Ø1.Ø SECS.

READY
SAVE
```
Program is stored as SQUART.

## EXERCISES

1.  Which of the following are valid numerical variable names?
    - A
    - B1
    - AB
    - A12
    - 3Z

Which of the following are valid string-variable names?

X
A$
2$
X$

2. Study the following program.

```
1Ø REM FIND AVERAGE OF FIVE NUMBERS
2Ø LET X = 1Ø9 + 375 + 97 + 271 + 592
3Ø LET A$ = "AVERAGE IS"
4Ø PRINT A$, X/5
5Ø END
```

Find examples of:

    Sequence number
    String Constant
    Numerical Constant
    String-Variable Name
    Numerical-Variable Name
    Arithmetic Operator
    Assignment Statement
    Program-Control Statement
    Input/Output Statement

3. Enter and run the program SQUART on your system. You will have to read about the operation of your terminal and your system's executive commands first or have someone show you how this job can be done.

   Next, change the SQUART program so that it will print the square root of all *even* numbers from 2 to 20. Enter and run the new program on your terminal.

   Finally, experiment! Try making mistakes and correcting them. Try entering the program statements in some other sequence. (Remember, BASIC uses the sequence numbers to determine the order of statement execution.) Try giving some name other than A to the numerical variable in the program.

4. Enter and run the following program to see if your system allows a digit as the second character of a string-variable name.

```
1Ø LET A1$ = "HELLO"
2Ø PRINT A1$
3Ø END
```

   If A1$ is allowed, your program will print "HELLO." If not, BASIC will tell you you've made a syntax error.

5. BASIC's automatic handling of number formats means you don't have to worry about how many places there are to the right or left of the decimal point. BASIC shifts from decimal to exponential format and back again as necessary. To understand better how BASIC handles output, feed ten numbers of varying sizes and formats into this small program:

```
1Ø LET C = Ø
2Ø INPUT N
3Ø PRINT N
4Ø LET C = C+1
5Ø IF C<1Ø THEN 2Ø
6Ø END
```

The program will cause a question mark to be displayed on your terminal. Enter a number in response to this query.

### FOOTNOTES AND REFERENCES

1  Generally, program names and data-file names can be from one to six alphamerical characters (A–Z, 0–9) in length. Some systems allow more characters and the use of special characters (for example, #, $), but you will always be safe if you stay within the six alphanumeric character limitation.

Xerox Data Systems software requires that file names also be enclosed in slashes—/FILE/. Peter Deutsch, one of the early developers of XDS (then SDS) 940 software at the University of California, once told me that he instituted these slashes as a temporary solution to a bug while he went on to larger problems. Before he could return to the file-name problem, however, he found the use of slashes had proliferated and been accepted across the country.

2  A discussion of constants and variables is included in Gear, section 3.1, "Assignment Statements."

3  The representation of numbers *inside* the computer is discussed by Gear in his sections 2.5.1, "Integers," 2.5.2, "Fixed Point Numbers," and 2.5.3, "Floating Point Numbers."

## THE REPLACEMENT OPERATOR

In chapter 3 we said that in BASIC the equal sign can mean replaced by, as in the statement

$$4\emptyset \quad \text{LET} \quad A \ = \ A \ + \ B$$

This works because the *value* of the expression A + B is being stored in the computer memory *location* labeled with the variable name A.[1] Thus the sequence

$$1\emptyset \quad \text{LET} \quad B \ = \ 1$$
$$2\emptyset \quad \text{LET} \quad A \ = \ B$$
$$3\emptyset \quad \text{LET} \quad A \ = \ A \ + \ B$$

produces the following images in the primary storage area:

| | | | |
|---|---|---|---|
| LET B = 1 | Memory | | 1 |
| | Label | A | B |
| LET A = B | Memory | 1 | 1 |
| | Label | A | B |
| LET A = A + B | Memory | 2 | 1 |
| | Label | A | B |

We cannot, however, replace the *value of an expression* with another *value*. LET A + B = C + 1 is an invalid statement (although, as will be illustrated in chapter 6, these values can be *compared*—IF A + B = C + 1 THEN 2$\emptyset$ is permissible).

## LETTING GO OF LET

Direct assignment of a value to a variable is accomplished by the LET statement in the form

LET variable = expression

LET can calculate, as well as assign, values. Statements that *read* values into locations cannot perform calculations. You'll learn more about these statements in the next chapter.

Chapter

# 4

# Assigning Values to Variables

Examples:

```
1Ø LET C = SQR(A + B)
2Ø LET C$ = "SQUARE OF SUM"
```

In early versions of BASIC this was the only method for assigning values directly. Most systems have now dropped LET as a required format word, however, and accept the simpler forms

```
1Ø C = SQR(A + B)
2Ø C$ = "SQUARE OF SUM"
```

You can determine with the following short program whether this ability has been incorporated into the BASIC compiler of your installation.

```
1Ø A = 1
2Ø PRINT A
3Ø END
RUNNH
```

If 1 is printed, LET is not required.

Now let's use LET statements to do a loan repayment calculation. A man borrows $1300 from a bank at 6% interest. He agrees to pay off the debt with twelve equal monthly payments. What will his monthly payment be? (Try flowcharting a solution before you look at the program.)

```
1Ø REM MONTHLY PAYMENT CALCULATION
2Ø LET P1 = 13ØØ
3Ø LET I = P1*.Ø6
4Ø LET P2 = P1 + I
5Ø LET M = P2/12
6Ø PRINT M
7Ø END

RUNNH


114.833

DONE
```

After you read about arithmetic operators in the rest of this chapter, you should be able to combine statements 20, 30, 40, and 50 into a single LET statement.

## ARITHMETIC OPERATORS[2]

The arithmetic or computational operators used in BASIC are

↑    exponentiation; A↑4 means $A^4$ or A to the fourth power
*    multiplication; A*B means $A \cdot B$ or $A \times B$ or A times B

/    division; A/B means $\dfrac{A}{B}$ or $A \div B$ or A divided by B

+    addition
−    subtraction

These arithmetic operators are used in combination with numerical variables, numerical constants, functions such as SQR, and parentheses to form *mathematical expressions*. Such expressions are used in calculations and comparison operations.

Note: A single numerical variable or a single constant can also be considered a very simple expression. All of the entries to the right of the replacement operator (=) in the following statements are mathematical expressions:

```
1Ø LET A = 1ØØ + X - Y + SQR(3*Z)
2Ø LET B = X
3Ø LET C = 3
```

### Rules of Precedence

An expression containing several BASIC functions and arithmetic operators could be construed in more than one way. For example, $4 + 3 + 5 * 2$ could equal 17, 20, or 24 depending on which operations are executed first.

Where there is no ambiguity, as in the $4 + 3$ part of the example, operations are performed from left to right. Where there is ambiguity (do we add or multiply first in the $3 + 5 * 2$ part of our expression?), BASIC assigns the following rules of precedence:

- Functions are performed first
- Exponentiation is performed next
- Multiplication and division are performed next
- Addition and subtraction are performed last
- When operators of equal precedence (such as multiplication and division) appear in the same expression, the leftmost is performed first.

Example:
  SQR(4) + 2Ø − 16/2↑3   Perform function first

    2    + 2Ø − 16/2↑3   No ambiguity; left-to-right rule applies

22   − 16/2↑3   Perform exponentiation next,

22   − 16/ 8   then division,

22   −   2   then subtraction.

20

Parentheses can be used to clarify or override the rules of precedence. Operations enclosed in parentheses are performed before the operations that surround them. Within parentheses the usual precedence and left-to-right rules apply.

Example:

| *Without Parentheses* | *With Parentheses* |
|---|---|
| 15/3 + 9*8 | 15/(3 + 9*8) |
| 5  +  72 | 15/(3 + 72) |
| 77 | 15/75 |
|  | .2 |

When parentheses enclose other parentheses, the operation within the innermost set is performed first.

Example:

4↑3 − SQR(13 + (8/2*3))

64 − SQR(13 + (8/2*3))

64 − SQR(13 +   12)

64 − SQR(25)

64 − 5

59

No two operators can appear consecutively. Parentheses can be used to separate them.

Example:

X/−3 is illegal.

X/(−3) is correct.

Return now to the monthly payment example shown earlier in this chapter. Can you combine the four LET statements into a single calculation? Check your results by running both programs.

### The Unary Minus

The last example above contains a unary minus, a minus sign that is not preceded by a constant or variable. The unary minus can present a special problem in determining the order of precedence in mathematical expressions. Consider, for example, the sequence

$A = -4$
$B = -A\uparrow2$

Most BASIC systems perform the unary minus calculation before exponentiation so that the product of this sequence is 16. In some systems, however, the unary minus has the same precedence as the binary minus (subtraction). In this case, the result of our problem would be $-16$. Test the operational sequence used by your BASIC compiler with a short program such as:

```
1Ø  REM UNARY MINUS PRECEDENCE TEST
2Ø  LET A = -4
3Ø  LET B = -A↑2
4Ø  PRINT B
5Ø  END
```

### EXERCISES

1.  Assume the value of A is 8,
         the value of B is 16,
      and the value of C is 3.

     | 8 | |16| | 3 | | |
     |---|---|---|
     | A | B | C | X |

     What will be the value of X after each of these instructions is executed?
     *a.*   1Ø LET X = A/SQR(B)∗4 − C↑2
     *b.*   3Ø LET X = A/SQR(B)∗(4 − C)↑2
     *c.*   7Ø LET X = A/SQR(B∗4) − C↑2

2.  Run the program shown in the section *"Letting Go of LET"* to determine whether your BASIC compiler allows you to drop LET from the assignment statement.

3.  How does your BASIC system handle the unary minus? Enter the program shown under *"Unary Minus"* above to find out.

4.  Calculate the *area* and the *circumference* of a rectangle.
     *a.*   Assign some value (the length) to L
     *b.*   Assign some value (the width) to W
     *c.*   Calculate and assign the area to A
     *d.*   Calculate and assign the circumference to C
     *e.*   PRINT "AREA IS" A
     *f.*   PRINT "CIRCUMFERENCE IS" C
     *g.*   END

(One possible solution is given in appendix B.)

5.  Flowchart and enter a program to calculate and print the circumference of a circle whose radius is 6 inches ($C = 2\pi R$). If your system has the pre-defined constant PI, use it. If not, use the value $\pi = 3.1416$.

## FOOTNOTES AND REFERENCES

1   Gear, section 3.2, "Data Types."
2   Gear, section 3.1, "Assignment Statements," includes a discussion of arithmetic operators and their precedence.

## PROGRAM INPUT

The LET statement allowed us to assign values to variables directly. Values can also be assigned to variables indirectly, by using the two BASIC input statements, READ and INPUT. The READ statement requires that the input values be built into the program in the form of DATA statements. INPUT accepts data entered at the terminal during program execution.

### The READ and DATA Statements

READ assigns values from one or more DATA statements to variables listed in the READ statement. The formats of these statements are

    READ variable, variable, . . . , variable
        .
        .
        .
    DATA value, value, . . . , value

For example,

    READ A,B,C,D,E
    DATA 10,9,8,7,1

is equivalent to the statements

    LET A=10
    LET B=9
    LET C=8
    LET D=7
    LET E=1

In this example the READ statement contains the same number of variables as the DATA statement has values, although this need not be the case. The following sequences achieve the same result:

# INPUT/OUTPUT

```
READ A
READ B
READ C,D,E
DATA 10,9,8,7,1,5,4

READ A,B,C,D,E
DATA 10,9,8
DATA 7,1,2,3
```

When it reads your program, BASIC saves all the values from all your DATA statements in statement number sequence. When a READ statement is encountered, the appropriate number of values are moved from this DATA list to the variables mentioned in the READ statement. The next time a READ statement is encountered, the read continues from the point where it was halted previously. In the examples above, the read pointer would be positioned at the number following 1 after the READ statements are executed. You must be careful to arrange your DATA values so they'll be read in the exact sequence you intend.

If a READ statement is encountered after all of the values in all the DATA statements have been used, the computer displays the message

OUT OF DATA

and the program terminates.

Any number of READ and DATA statements can appear in a program; if one of these statements is present, however, there must be at least one occurrence of the counterpart. Generally speaking, the only limit to the number of entries in a READ or DATA statement is the length of the input line (the terminal carriage length).

In the program on the next page, RAIN1, DATA statements are used to supply the total amount of rainfall for the months of the year. The program prints the amount of rainfall for each month, the total for the year, and the monthly average.

As this example indicates, DATA values can be numerical or string. Numerical DATA values can be in integer (3, 12), decimal (3.4, 12.1), or exponential (4.3E15—equivalent to 4.3 times $10^{15}$) form, but mathematical expressions such as 10/7 or (25↑2 + 3) will befuddle your computer's limited imagination. READ/DATA statements are less versatile than LET in this respect.

To find the average rainfall for another year, the program can be reentered with new values in statements 150–170. If the program has been saved by the system, then only the three DATA statements need be reentered.

## The RESTORE Statement

RESTORE causes the next READ statement to return to the first value contained in the first DATA statement. It is commonly used when more than one calculation must be performed on the same data.

```
1Ø REM T = TOTAL FOR YEAR
2Ø LET T = Ø
3Ø READ M$, A
4Ø PRINT M$; A; "INCHES"
5Ø REM ADD TO TOTAL
6Ø LET T = T + A
7Ø REM AT END  GO TO 11Ø
8Ø IF M$ = "DEC" THEN 11Ø
9Ø REM IF NOT END, GO TO 3Ø
1ØØ GOTO 3Ø
11Ø PRINT "TOTAL FOR YEAR" T
12Ø REM CALCULATE AVERAGE
13Ø LET T2 = T/12
14Ø PRINT "AVERAGE MONTHLY RAINFALL" T2
15Ø DATA "JAN", 3.2, "FEB", 2.1, "MAR", 1.9, "APR", 2.6
16Ø DATA "MAY", 1.6, "JUN", 1.1, "JUL", 1.2, "AUG", 1.1
17Ø DATA "SEP", 1.9, "OCT", 3.2, "NOV", 4.7, "DEC", 5.2
18Ø END
RUNNH
```

```
JAN 3.2          INCHES
FEB 2.1          INCHES
MAR 1.9          INCHES
APR 2.6          INCHES
MAY 1.6          INCHES
JUN 1.1          INCHES
JUL 1.2          INCHES
AUG 1.1          INCHES
SEP 1.9          INCHES
OCT 3.2          INCHES
NOV 4.7          INCHES
DEC 5.2          INCHES
TOTAL FOR YEAR 29.8
AVERAGE MONTHLY RAINFALL 2.48333
```

DONE

The LET, READ, and DATA statements all consist of a *keyword* (LET, READ, DATA) followed by one or more *arguments* (an expression, value, or other parameter). The RESTORE statement differs in that it uses no arguments. (See next page.)

Note that you need not read all data before restoring. Data can be reread as often as the RESTORE statement is encountered in the program.

### INPUT—Entering Data During Program Execution

READ and DATA provide a means of entering data values at the time a program is being entered and of saving the data with the program. Large amounts of input data can be handled using these statements. At times, however, we want to enter the data when the program is executing. For example:

```
1Ø  READ A,B,C                    (A=1Ø, B=3.7, C=16)
2Ø  REM FIRST CALCULATION
 •
 •
 •
9Ø  RESTORE
1ØØ  READ X,Y
11Ø  REM SECOND CALCULATION       (X=1Ø, Y=3.7)
 •
 •
 •
19Ø  RESTORE
2ØØ  READ Q,R,S                   (Q=1Ø, R=3.7, S=16)
21Ø  REM THIRD CALCULATION
 •
 •
3ØØ  DATA 1Ø, 3.7, 16, 6.22E8
31Ø  END
```

- In games and in computer-aided instruction, we want to respond to each new problem as it arises. Putting our responses into a DATA statement would be like writing down all our moves in a chess match before our opponent sets up his pieces.
- We often need to use generalized programs over and over again, with different data each time. For example, our rainfall averaging program could be reused every year with new input data. If the program logic is complex, or if the program user is not a programmer, it may not be practical to change and recompile the program every time new data is needed.
- Or, in general, the terminal user may want to see the output calculated in earlier program steps before he enters more data.

This ability to enter data while the program is executing is provided by the INPUT statement.

The format of the INPUT statement is

INPUT variable, variable, . . . , variable

When the statement is executed, BASIC displays a question mark on the terminal and waits for the user to enter a value for each variable listed in the INPUT statement. Your data, entered in response to one INPUT statement, must be entered on one input line with entries separated by commas. The carriage return signals the end of your input.

Note that INPUT data can be numerical (statement 30) or string (statement 70). Numerical INPUT, like numerical values in a DATA statement, can be in integer, decimal, or exponential format.

```
1Ø REM FIND THE AVERAGE OF FIVE NUMBERS
2Ø PRINT "ENTER FIVE NUMBERS"
3Ø INPUT A,B,C,D,E
4Ø LET X = (A+B+C+D+E)/5
5Ø PRINT "AVERAGE IS" X
6Ø PRINT "MORE? TYPE Y OR N"
7Ø INPUT R$
8Ø IF R$ = "Y" THEN 2Ø
9Ø END
RUNNH
```

```
ENTER FIVE NUMBERS
?7, 1Ø, 3, -12, 1.5
AVERAGE IS 1.9
MORE? TYPE Y OR N
?Y
ENTER FIVE NUMBERS
?17, 3.6, 42, 1.Ø74, 6.3E7
AVERAGE IS 1.26ØØØE+Ø7
MORE? TYPE Y OR N
?N
```

DONE

If you are designing a program that will call for input from its user, usually you should print a message before each INPUT statement. The message describes the kind of response you expect from the user. Statements 20 and 60 in the last example illustrate this practice.

If the user enters too few values in response to the question mark, the system issues an error message and allows him to try again.

## PROGRAM OUTPUT

### The PRINT Statement

Data output in BASIC is performed by the PRINT statement. PRINT not only prints data on your terminal, but also lets you determine the format of the output.

The simplest form of the PRINT statement uses no arguments. The statement

```
5Ø PRINT
```

skips one line on the output sheet. To skip more lines, repeat the instruction.

```
6Ø PRINT
7Ø PRINT
```

**Printing Numbers**    To print the value of a previously calculated or assigned variable, use the form,

PRINT variable

Example :

```
1Ø LET A = 3
2Ø LET B = 4*A+2
3Ø PRINT A
4Ø PRINT
5Ø PRINT B
6Ø END
RUNNH
```


<u>3</u>


<u>14</u>

<u>DONE</u>


You can print the value of any expression using PRINT.

```
1Ø LET A = 3
2Ø PRINT A
3Ø PRINT A↑2+6
4Ø PRINT 1ØØ
5Ø END
RUNNH
```


<u>3</u>
<u>15</u>
<u>1ØØ</u>

<u>DONE</u>


To print more than one item on the same line, use commas or semicolons to separate the variables :

```
1Ø  READ A,B,C,D
2Ø  PRINT A,B,C
3Ø  PRINT
4Ø  PRINT
5Ø  PRINT A;B;C;D
6Ø  DATA 5, 6, 7, 8
7Ø  END
RUNNH
```

   <u>5</u>                      <u>6</u>                    <u>7</u>

   <u>5</u>      <u>6</u>      <u>7</u>      <u>8</u>

<u>DONE</u>

The comma and semicolon are tabulating features built into the PRINT statement. They provide the simplest form of print format control. Another example, with statement 10 indicating print positions, will clarify the effects of this punctuation.

```
1Ø  PRINT "123456789 123456789 123456789 123456789"
2Ø  READ A,B,C,D,E,F,G
3Ø  READ A1,B1,C1,D1
4Ø  READ H,I,J
5Ø  PRINT A;B,C;D
6Ø  PRINT E,F,G
7Ø  PRINT A1;B1,C1;D1
8Ø  PRINT D;H;I;J
9Ø  DATA 1,2,3,4,5,6,7
1ØØ DATA -1,-2,-3,-4
11Ø DATA 45,-456,4567
12Ø END
RUNNH
```

<u>123456789</u> <u>123456789</u> <u>123456789</u> <u>123456789</u>
 <u>1</u>        <u>2</u>           <u>3</u>       <u>4</u>
 <u>5</u>                   <u>6</u>                <u>7</u>
<u>-1</u>     <u>-2</u>      <u>-3</u>     <u>-4</u>
 <u>4</u>     <u>45</u>    <u>-456</u>   <u>4567</u>

<u>DONE</u>

The terminal line is divided into five zones, each fifteen spaces wide. *Comma tabs* are set every fifteen spaces at print positions 16, 31, 46, and 61 — hence the output from printing statement 60 above, where the variables are separated by commas.

*Semicolon tabs* are set three spaces apart. A semicolon causes the next item to be printed at the next semicolon tab. If this tab is less than three spaces away, it is skipped and the following semicolon tab is used. Thus semicolon punctuation ensures that you will have at least three blanks between the items printed.

You may have observed some apparent discrepancies between the last example and what has just been said about comma tabs. The output from statement 60 of our example appears in print positions 2, 17, and 32 instead of at the assigned comma tabs. The explanation is that BASIC allows one space for a number's sign. If the sign is positive ( + ), the space is left blank; if negative ( − ), the minus is printed. A position is also left for the sign when using semicolon tabs.

Comma tabs are useful for printing tables. The following program prints a table listing the square, cube, and fourth power of the numbers 20–22.

```
10 READ A,B,C
20 PRINT "NUMBER", "SQUARED", "CUBED", "TO THE FOURTH"
30 PRINT
40 PRINT A, A↑2, A↑3, A↑4
50 PRINT B, B↑2, B↑3, B↑4
60 PRINT C, C↑2, C↑3, C↑4
70 DATA 20, 21, 22
80 END
RUNNH
```

| NUMBER | SQUARED | CUBED | TO THE FOURTH |
|--------|---------|-------|---------------|
| 20 | 400 | 8000 | 160000. |
| 21 | 441 | 9261 | 194481. |
| 22 | 484 | 10648 | 234256. |

DONE

Semicolon punctuation is useful when you want to print many numbers on the same line. The program on the next page multiplies any given number by the values 1 through 12. If a user inputs his monthly salary, the output will be a month-by-month accounting of his accumulated earnings for one year.

If a PRINT command contains too much data for one line, the printing continues on a new line.

Normally the terminal carriage skips to the beginning of a new line after a PRINT is executed. If you want the printout to continue on the same line, add a comma or semicolon after the last item in the PRINT statement.

```
1Ø  PRINT "ENTER A NUMBER"
2Ø  INPUT X
3Ø  PRINT X;2*X;3*X;4*X;5*X;6*X;7*X;8*X;9*X;1Ø*X;11*X;12*X
4Ø  END
RUNNH
```

ENTER A NUMBER
?525

| 525 | 1Ø5Ø | 1575 | 21ØØ | 2625 | 315Ø | 3675 | 42ØØ |
|-----|------|------|------|------|------|------|------|
| 4725 | 525Ø | 5775 | 63ØØ | | | | |

DONE

```
1Ø   PRINT 1,2
2Ø   PRINT 3;4;
3Ø   PRINT 5
4Ø   PRINT "FINISHED"
5Ø   END
RUNNH
```

| 1 | | 2 |
|---|---|---|
| 3 | 4 | 5 |

FINISHED

DONE

**Printing Strings**    As we have already seen in several examples, the PRINT statement can also be used to print string constants and string variables.

```
1Ø   PRINT "1,2,3"
2Ø   LET H$="HELLO"
3Ø   PRINT H$
4Ø   END
RUNNH
```

1,2,3
HELLO

DONE

To combine both variable and literal output, use the PRINT statement as in the SQUART example.

```
3Ø PRINT "THE SQUARE ROOT OF" A "IS" SQR(A)
```

In the table-printing example, commas were used to tabulate strings as well as numbers.

```
2Ø PRINT "NUMBER", "SQUARED", "CUBED", "TO THE FOURTH"
```

When a semicolon is used after string output, however, no spacing or tabulation occurs, except for the normal spacing for the sign of a number.

The following program, WEIGHT, converts pounds to kilograms. Note the use of the semicolon in statement 20 to ensure that the user's input will be printed on the same line as the word POUNDS.

```
1Ø    REM CONVERT POUNDS TO KILOGRAMS
2Ø    PRINT "POUNDS";
3Ø    INPUT P
4Ø    REM ONE KG = 2.2 LBS
5Ø    LET K=P/2.2
6Ø    PRINT "KILOGRAMS:";K
7Ø    PRINT
8Ø    GOTO 1Ø
9Ø    END
RUNNH


POUNDS?4
KILOGRAMS: 1.81818


POUNDS?27.75
KILOGRAMS: 12.6136

POUNDS?16.125
KILOGRAMS: 7.32955
S
```

**The TAB Function**   TAB is a BASIC formatting function available with most systems. It is used with PRINT to specify the exact print position desired.

```
5Ø PRINT A;TAB(12) "TOTAL"
```

After the value of the variable A is printed, the terminal spaces to print position 12 and types TOTAL.

Note that A is followed by a semicolon. If it had been followed by a comma, BASIC would have spaced to position 16 before noticing the TAB(12) request. In general, the TAB statement is ineffectual whenever the terminal has passed the print position specified as TAB's argument. Using a semicolon reduces the risk of the TAB function being bypassed.

**A General Comment on Formatting Output**   Spacing of printed output may seem confusing. Some systems have their own rules and quirks to add to the confusion. But don't worry, you'll soon know how to get the printout you want. When you're writing a simple program to do a few calculations for yourself, you're not usually concerned with the precise format of your output. If your program is to create a table or report, you can experiment with test data to be sure that the printout is clear.

## EXERCISES

1. Write a program to calculate the average of five numbers. (See exercise 2 in chapter 3.) Let the program READ the five numbers from a DATA statement. After you have tested the program, change the DATA statement to find the average of five new numbers.

2. Rewrite your averaging program (exercise 1) so that it INPUTs the five numbers instead of READing them. Be sure to have a PRINT statement (indicating that five numbers are expected) before the INPUT statement. Run the program several times; enter different numbers each time.

3. Write a program that asks the user his name and then prints (on one line) the word "HELLO" followed by a space and the user's name.

4. Write a program that calculates the circumference (4 × edge), the surface area (6 × edge$^2$), and the volume (edge$^3$) of four cubes. The length of the edges of the four cubes are 2.5, 3.5, 4.1, and 6.2. Use READ and DATA to enter the lengths of the edges. Print the results in a table with the following headings across the top:

   EDGE            CIRCUMFERENCE SURFACE        VOLUME

   First test your program by placing one-digit values in the DATA statement so that you can easily verify the results. Then reenter the DATA statement with the required values.

BASIC program instructions are normally executed in sequence by statement number. Program-control statements allow you to alter the execution sequence or to stop execution.

There are three categories of program-control statements: branching, loop control, and program terminators. GOTO and IF—THEN statements are used for branching, FOR and NEXT statements for loop control, and STOP and END to terminate program execution.

## BRANCHING OPERATIONS[1]

### The GOTO Statement

GOTO is the most straightforward of the branching statements. It uses the form

GOTO statement-number

The statement

```
140 GOTO 80
```

means branch immediately to statement 80, no questions asked!

The program shown on the following page calculates and prints the square roots of all positive integers.

Instructions 20—40 are called a "loop," because they are executed repeatedly. Note that in this example there is no way to leave the loop once it is entered. The loop is called an *endless loop*. The user will have to interfere in order to terminate program execution. All systems have some convention by which the user can "cancel" a program (for example, entering an S). Be sure you know how it is done on your system. You will want to cancel a program when you see that its logic is incorrect or when (intentionally or not) you have coded an endless loop.

### The IF—THEN Statement

The GOTO statement causes your program to branch unconditionally. In many cases, how-

```
1Ø LET X = Ø
2Ø LET X = X + 1
3Ø PRINT "THE SQUARE ROOT OF" X "IS" SQR(X)
4Ø GOTO 2Ø
5Ø END
RUNNH
```

| THE SQUARE ROOT OF 1 | IS 1 |
|---|---|
| THE SQUARE ROOT OF 2 | IS 1.41421 |
| THE SQUARE ROOT OF 3 | IS 1.73205 |
| THE SQUARE ROOT OF 4 | IS 2 |
| THE SQUARE ROOT OF 5 | IS 2.23607 |
| THE SQUARE ROOT OF 6 | IS 2.44949 |

S

ever, you will want to branch only if a particular condition is met; for example, if a counter has reached a certain value.

Conditional branching is controlled by the IF—THEN statement, which has the format

IF relational-expression THEN statement number

The "relational expression" part of the IF—THEN statement compares mathematical expressions or literals using the following relational operators:

| | |
|---|---|
| $=$ | equal to |
| $<$ | less than |
| $=<$ or $<=$ | less than or equal to |
| $>$ | greater than |
| $=>$ or $>=$ | greater than or equal to |
| $<>$ | not equal |

Examples:

```
1Ø IF A*B-7 = 1Ø THEN 11Ø
```
> If A*B—7 equals 10, statement 110 is executed next.

```
4Ø IF Z9 >= 22 THEN 12Ø
```
> If the value of the variable Z9 exceeds or equals 22, statement 120 is executed next.

```
6Ø IF M$ = "JANUARY" THEN 13Ø
```
> If the string variable M$ contains the characters JANUARY, statement 130 is executed next.

90  IF  B↑2  -  C↑2  =  Ø  THEN  14Ø
>If $B^2 - C^2$ is zero, statement 140 is executed next.

In statements like the first example above, where both arithmetic and relational operators are present, the arithmetic operations are performed in the sequence described in chapter 4 and then the relational comparison is made. In all of the examples, if the specified relationship is "true," control passes to the indicated statement. If the relationship is "false" (not true), execution continues with the statement following the IF—THEN statement.

Now you have learned all the instructions needed to solve the *Indian Problem*. In 1626 the Indians sold the island of Manhattan for $24. Had this money been placed in a savings account at 3% interest at that time, what would it amount to today?

The solution to this problem uses INPUT to enter the current year, LET to initialize and increment a counter and to calculate the principal, IF—THEN to control the calculation loop, GOTO to perpetuate the loop, and PRINT to display the final principal.

```
1Ø  REM  INDIAN  PROBLEM
2Ø  PRINT  "ENTER  CURRENT  YEAR"
3Ø  INPUT  Y
4Ø  REM  INITIALIZE  COUNTER
5Ø  LET  C  =  1626
6Ø  REM  INITIALIZE  PRINCIPAL  AMOUNT
7Ø  LET  P  =  24.ØØ
8Ø  REM  BEGIN  CALCULATION  LOOP
9Ø  LET  P  =  P  +  P*.Ø3
1ØØ LET  C  =  C+1
11Ø IF  C  =  Y  THEN  13Ø
12Ø GOTO  9Ø
13Ø REM  DISPLAY  RESULTS
14Ø PRINT  P
15Ø END
RUNNH


ENTER  CURRENT  YEAR
?1972
  663578.

DONE
```

What statement would you insert to print yearly interim results? How would you format the printout to conserve space? How would you change statements 50, 100, and 110 to initialize the counter with the current year and decrement it until 1626 is reached? How would you use READ and DATA to accomplish the same result as statement 50?

## LOOP CONTROL (FOR AND NEXT)

While the GOTO and IF—THEN statements are generally classified as branching instructions, they can also be used to loop repeatedly through a series of statements. We used IF—THEN in this way in the Indian problem. Coding is often simplified, however, if FOR and NEXT are used for loop control instead of IF—THEN or GOTO.[2]

The FOR statement is placed at the beginning of a loop, the NEXT statement at the end. FOR names a numerical variable that is to be incremented each time the loop is executed. It gives the initial value of the variable, the increment, and the final value.

> FOR variable = initial TO final STEP increment
> .
> .
> .
> NEXT variable

Example:

```
9Ø   FOR C = 1626 TO Y-1 STEP 1
1ØØ  LET P = P + P*.Ø3
11Ø  NEXT C
```

These three statements perform the same functions as statements 50, 90, 100, 110, and 120 of the Indian program.

Statements between FOR and NEXT are executed initially with the variable set to its initial value. Then the increment is added to the variable and the loop is executed again. The process is repeated until addition of the increment causes the variable to exceed its final value. Control then passes to the statement following the NEXT statement.

The variable in the FOR statement must be numerical and must be identical to the variable in the NEXT statement to make clear which loop the NEXT is terminating. The initial value, the final value, and the increment can be mathematical expressions, but the entire FOR statement cannot exceed one input line. STEP and "increment" can be omitted, in which case a value of $+1$ is assumed. For example, statement 90 above could have been written

```
9Ø FOR C = 1626 TO Y-1
```

Note that the values in the FOR statement need not be positive and need not be integers. Obviously, the increment should not be zero, but it can be negative, in which case it becomes a decrement.

```
5Ø  FOR Z = 1Ø TO -1Ø STEP -2
```

FOR–NEXT loops can have other FOR–NEXT loops imbedded in them. Control loops through the *inner* FOR–NEXT, using all of its specified variable values, each time the *outer* FOR–NEXT is performed.

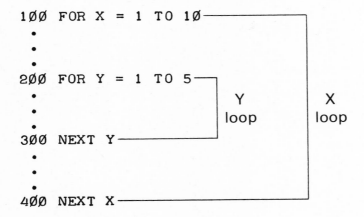

```
1ØØ  FOR X = 1 TO 1Ø
  •
  •
  •
2ØØ  FOR Y = 1 TO 5
  •
  •
  •
3ØØ  NEXT Y
  •
  •
  •
4ØØ  NEXT X
```

Y loop     X loop

The X loop is executed ten times. The Y loop is executed fifty times— five times each time the X loop is executed.

The following program, TRAREA, calculates the area of a triangle (base times ½ the perpendicular height) as the base varies from 5 to 15 (in two-unit increments) and the height varies from 3 to 10 (in increments of one unit).

$$\text{Area} = \frac{BH}{2}$$

H

B

```
1Ø  FOR B = 5 TO 15 STEP 2
2Ø  FOR H = 3 TO 1Ø
3Ø  PRINT "B =" B; "H =" H; "AREA IS" B*H/2
4Ø  NEXT H
5Ø  NEXT B
6Ø  END
RUNNH
```

This program continues on the next page.

| | | | |
|---|---|---|---|
| B = 5 | H = 3 | AREA IS | 7.5 |
| B = 5 | H = 4 | AREA IS | 10 |
| B = 5 | H = 5 | AREA IS | 12.5 |
| B = 5 | H = 6 | AREA IS | 15 |
| B = 5 | H = 7 | AREA IS | 17.5 |
| B = 5 | H = 8 | AREA IS | 20 |
| B = 5 | H = 9 | AREA IS | 22.5 |
| B = 5 | H = 10 | AREA IS | 25 |
| B = 7 | H = 3 | AREA IS | 10.5 |
| B = 7 | H = 4 | AREA IS | 14 |

etc.

First, statements 10 and 20 are executed (B=5, H=3). Statements 20 and 40 cause statement 30 to be executed repeatedly (with the value of B remaining constant while H varies from 3 to 10 in increments of 1). When H exceeds its terminal value (10), control passes to statement 50 causing B to be incremented by 2, and the entire procedure begins again. The program ends when the calculation has been performed with B=15 and H=10.

Note that the H loop is entirely inside, or legally nested within the B loop.

An error message is issued if FOR—NEXT loops overlap, as below.

A FOR—NEXT loop, nested within another FOR—NEXT loop, using the same variable as the outer loop is also an error.

## PROGRAM TERMINATION

BASIC provides two program terminators—STOP and END.

### The STOP Statement

The STOP statement, in effect, is a branch to the statement containing END. It can be used to provide more than one logical termination point in a program. The format of the STOP statement is simply the keyword STOP, with no argument.

```
1ØØ  STOP
```

There can be as many STOP statements in a program as are needed. In the following example, STOP is used to terminate processing when an error occurs (B=Ø is considered an error in this program segment).

- •
- •
- •

```
1ØØ  IF B <> Ø THEN 13Ø
11Ø  PRINT "B = Ø; PROCESSING CANNOT CONTINUE"
12Ø  STOP
13Ø  LET C = A/B
```

- •
- •
- •

```
2ØØ  END
```

## The END Statement

Every BASIC program must have one, and only one, END statement, and it must be the statement with the highest sequence number. END tells the BASIC compiler where to stop program compilation. It also terminates execution of the program.

Like STOP, the END statement uses no arguments.

## EXERCISES

1. Flowchart and enter a program that tells how much money an investor will have if he invests D dollars at P % interest for Y years. (Interest is compounded annually.)
   - a. Ask the investor how much money he has to invest.
   - b. Ask him what percentage of interest he gets.
   - c. Ask him how many years he will leave the money invested.
   - d. Multiply the percentage by the amount and add the interest to the dollars invested. Be sure to divide the percentage amount by 100.
   - e. Add 1 to some counter used to keep track of how many years the money has been invested.
   - f. If the calculation in step *d* has not yet been performed Y times, return to step *d*.
   - g. Print the final dollar amount.

2. Add instructions at the end of the investment program to ask the investor if he would like to perform another investment calculation. Depending on his response, return to step *a* or terminate the program.

3. Modify the program to ask the investor how much money he has to invest, what interest percentage he will get, and how much money he would like

to have. Let your program tell him how many years he will have to leave the money invested.

4. Flowchart and enter a program to test a student's knowledge of multiplication by 9. Assume a grade school student as your user. Ask him for the product of 9 times 1. Tell him if he is right or wrong. If he is wrong, tell him the correct answer. Continue the process for 9 times 2 through 9 times 10. At the end, if he answered all questions correctly, print VERY GOOD. If he had one error, print GOOD. If he had two or more errors, print TRY AGAIN and return to the start of the program.

5. Expand the same multiplication program to test the student's knowledge of the entire multiplication table, from 2 times 2 through 12 times 12. This will require an imbedded FOR—NEXT loop. The outside loop will increment the multiplicand from 2 through 12, and the inside loop will increment the multiplier from 2 through 12. This time print VERY GOOD if the student has less than three errors. Print GOOD if he has from three to five errors. Restart if he has six or more. (One possible solution is given in appendix B.)

§ 3.5  6.* Flowchart and enter a program that predicts the future population of a given area.
   a. Ask the program's user to enter:
      ● The present population of the area
      ● The birth rate
      ● The number of deaths during the previous year
      ● The current year
      ● The year for which the prediction is to be made
   b. Calculate the death rate based on this year's population and last year's deaths.
   c. Using FOR and NEXT, loop through a routine that repeatedly multiplies the birth rate times the previous year-end population and the death rate times the previous year-end population to get the new year-end population.
   d. Print the predicted population for the year requested.
   e. Test your program with the following (United States) data:
      ● Present population = 205.1 million
      ● Birth rate = 1.8%
      ● Deaths = 1,921,000
      ● Present year = 1971
      ● Predict for 1990

*This problem is discussed and flowcharted in Gear, section 3.5.

#### FOOTNOTES AND REFERENCES

1  Gear, section 3.4, "Program Logic."
2  Gear, section 3.5, "Program Loops," is a general discussion of looping. Section 5.1 is an excellent description of the FOR—NEXT operation.

Many specialized functions have been defined by scientists, engineers, and mathematicians to solve frequently occurring problems such as square root, absolute value, sine, cosine, and logarithm. To solve problems involving these functions, you would normally have to look up previously calculated results in tables or perform a power series expansion to arrive at an approximate solution.[1]

$$\exp(x) = 1 + x + x^2/2 + x^3/3 + \ldots$$
$$\cos(x) = 1 - x^2/2 + x^4/4 - x^6/6 + \ldots$$
$$\sin(x) = x - x^3/3 + x^5/5 - x^7/7 + \ldots$$

BASIC, however, simplifies all this for you. The last expansion, for example, can be solved in BASIC by the statement

### 40 LET S = SIN(X)

The original version of BASIC provided its users with ten predefined mathematical and utility functions.[2] These functions are covered in this chapter. You may find that additional predefined functions are offered in the particular system you're using.

BASIC also lets you define your own functions using the DEF statement. This feature is described at the end of the chapter.

## PREDEFINED FUNCTIONS

BASIC functions can generally be grouped into four categories: trigonometric, exponential, arithmetic, and utility. Each function consists of a three-letter name followed by an argument enclosed in parentheses. The argument is a mathematical expression, which means it can include other functions.

Examples:

```
SQR(9.765)
LOG(X)
SQR(D + E/4 + SQR(F + 7) +
    LOG(G*H))
```

### Trigonometric Functions

The BASIC trigonometric functions interpret the argument X as an angle measured in radians (one radian equals approximately 57°; there are $2\pi$ radians in a circle).

SIN(X)   The sine of X is calculated.
COS(X)   The cosine of X is calculated.
TAN(X)   The tangent of X is calculated.
ATN(X)   The arctangent of X is calculated (angle whose tangent is X);
the answer is in radians.

```
1Ø LET A = Ø.25
2Ø PRINT "SINE OF" A "IS" SIN(A)
3Ø PRINT "COSINE OF" A "IS" COS(A)
4Ø PRINT "TANGENT OF" A "IS" TAN(A)
5Ø PRINT "ARCTANGENT OF" A "IS" ATN(A)
6Ø END
RUNNH
```

```
SINE OF .25          IS .2474Ø4
COSINE OF .25         IS .968912
TANGENT OF .25        IS .255342
ARCTANGENT OF .25      IS .2449 79
```

DONE

How would you print your own sine table for angles in the 0—90 degree range, in increments of 1/10 degree? (Hint: convert a value D—degrees—to radians by calculating $D*\pi/18Ø$ or $D*3.14159265/18Ø$.)

### Exponential Functions

For exponential functions, the argument X can be any expression.

EXP(X)   The natural exponent of X ($e^x$) is calculated (e = 2.71828 . . .).
LOG(X)   The natural logarithm of X ($\log_e X$) is calculated.
SQR(X)   The square root of X ($X^{\frac{1}{2}}$ or $\sqrt{X}$) is calculated. X must be positive.

Enter and run the following short program.

```
1Ø INPUT A,B,C
2Ø PRINT "NATURAL EXPONENT OF" A "IS" EXP(A)
3Ø PRINT "NATURAL LOG OF" B "IS" LOG(B)
4Ø PRINT "SQUARE ROOT OF" C "IS" SQR(C)
5Ø END
RUNNH
```

```
?12,13,14
NATURAL EXPONENT OF 12    IS 162755.
NATURAL LOG OF 13    IS 2.56495
SQUARE ROOT OF 14    IS 3.74166

DONE
```

Now check the EXP function by performing the calculation

```
25 LET X = 2.71828↑A
26 PRINT X
```

### Arithmetic Functions

For arithmetic functions, the argument X can be any expression.

ABS(X)  Determines the absolute value of X ($|X|$).

SGN(X)  Determines the sign of X. The result is $+1$, $-1$, or 0. If X is positive, the result is $+1$; if X is negative, the result is $-1$; if X = 0, the result is 0.

INT(X)  Calculates the integer part of X ($[X]$). INT calculates the *largest integer not greater than X*. Thus the expression INT($-5.32$) gives the result $-6$.

```
INT(17.9) is 17
INT(−17.9) is −18
INT(17) is 17
```

The following program demonstrates the different effects of these functions.

```
1Ø    READ A,B,C
2Ø    PRINT "ABS VALUES OF"A;B;C"ARE"ABS(A);ABS(B);ABS(C)
3Ø    PRINT "INTEGER PARTS OF"A;B;C"ARE"INT(A);INT(B);INT(C)
4Ø    PRINT "SIGNS OF"A;B;C"ARE"SGN(A);SGN(B);SGN(C)
5Ø    DATA Ø,3Ø.67,-3.67
6Ø    END


RUNNH


ABS VALUES OF Ø      3Ø.67      -3.67      ARE Ø      3Ø.67
  3.67
INTEGER PARTS OF Ø      3Ø.67      -3.67      ARE Ø      3Ø    -4
SIGNS OF Ø      3Ø.67      -3.67      ARE Ø      1      -1

DONE
```

A frequent application of the integer function is to round numbers. To round a variable *n* to the nearest integer, calculate

INT(n + .5)

INT(17.4 + .5) is INT(17.9) equal to 17
INT(17.5 + .5) is INT(18) equal to 18
INT(17.61 + .5) is INT(18.11) equal to 18

To round a variable *n* to *d* decimal places, calculate

INT(n∗1Ø↑d + .5)/1Ø↑d

Example:

N = .2748
d = 3
INT(N∗1Ø↑3 + .5)/1Ø↑3 = .275

N = .274491
d = 3
INT(N∗1Ø↑3 + .5)/1Ø↑3 = .274

Perform this calculation yourself, supplying different values for *n* and *d*, until you understand why the formula works.

### Utility Functions

Most of the BASIC functions developed since the inception of the language are utilities. These include format-control functions, such as functions for returning the time and date, or for creating line numbers on data files. Only two utility functions have widespread application, however: TAB and RND.

TAB(X)    Used in PRINT statements to tabulate output. X specifies a print position. See chapter 5.
RND(X)    Returns a random number between 0 and 1.

Some systems do not require an argument after the function RND. Of those systems that require the argument, most ignore it. In this case, any constant will suffice. A few systems allow you to use the argument to control the starting point of random-number generation. For example, RND(1ØØ) might cause BASIC to go through 100 iterations of its random-number generating formula before it calculates a random number for you. If your system does not have this feature, you may find that you get the same random number every time you run your program. You can test the capabilities of your system with the following programs:

```
1Ø FOR N = 1 TO 1Ø
2Ø PRINT RND
3Ø NEXT N
4Ø END
```

If this program works, rerun it to see if the same ten numbers are printed. If it doesn't work, or if you do get the same numbers, try the next program.

```
1Ø PRINT "ENTER AN INTEGER"
2Ø INPUT X
3Ø FOR N = 1 TO 1Ø
4Ø PRINT RND(X)
5Ø NEXT N
6Ø END
```

If this program works, rerun it several times entering different integers and duplicating some.

RND can be combined with the INT function to obtain sets of random integers within specific number ranges. For example, to obtain 100 one-digit random integers we could enter the following program:

```
1Ø FOR N = 1 TO 1ØØ
2Ø PRINT INT(1Ø*RND(Ø));
3Ø NEXT N
4Ø END
```

Another useful formula involving INT lets you specify the upper and lower limits of your random integer range.

PRINT INT($n*$RND(Ø) + i);

where

n = the number of integers in your range
i = the lowest number in your range

For example, to specify that you want your random integers to range between 3 and 15 inclusive, enter:

```
2Ø PRINT INT(13*RND(Ø) + 3)
```

### USER-DEFINED FUNCTIONS (DEF)

Using BASIC's DEF statement, you can create functions to fit your own special situation, calling on them as often as you like in the course of running your program. The name of a user-defined function consists of three letters— FN plus one alphabetic character.

To illustrate the use of DEF, let's define a function (FNM) to convert inches to millimeters.

DEF FNM(I) = I/Ø.Ø4

If we include this definition in a program, we can use FNM to perform the inches-to-millimeters conversion as often as we like in the rest of the program.

We can code, for example:

    PRINT FNM(8.65)

instead of

    LET X = 8.65/0.04
    PRINT X

The following function calculates the cost of gasoline for a vacation trip. Dividing the total mileage (T) by our automobile's miles-per-gallon average (M) tells us how much gas will be used. Multiplying this result by the price per gallon (P) gives the total gasoline cost (C).

$$C = \left( \frac{T}{M} \right) P$$

```
10 DEF FNC(T,M,P) = T/M * P
20 INPUT T,M,P
30 PRINT "COST IS" FNC(T,M,P) "DCLLARS"
40 END
RUNNH


?1000, 20, 0.40
COST IS   20   DOLLARS
```

A 1000-mile trip requires $20 for gasoline if our car averages twenty miles per gallon and gasoline costs forty cents per gallon. To calculate the cost ratio using two different grades of gasoline, we might have a statement like the following:

```
60 PRINT FNC (T,M1,P1)/FNC(T,M2,P2)
```

where T, M1, P1, M2, and P2 are variables whose values have been assigned previously.

As can be seen in statement 10, the expression on the left side of the equal sign in a function definition specifies the function name (FNM, FNC) and variables (T, M, P). These variables are called *dummy variables* because they do not actually refer to locations in computer memory. They are used merely to hold the place of values to be inserted later. In the first gasoline-cost example, the dummy-variable names (T, M, P) are also used to name the actual variables evaluated by the function at statement 30. In the cost-ratio example, other variable names (M1, P1, M2, P2) are used. The number of dummy variables allowed in a single function definition varies with different systems (some allow only one).

The real heart of the function is the calculation to the right of the equal sign. This calculation is performed each time the function is called. It can contain all the ingredients of a regular BASIC expression, including other functions, variables defined elsewhere in the program, and subscripted variables (see chapter 9).

One function can call another, but an error results in most systems if recursion occurs (that is, a function may not call itself or another function that references the calling function).

Illegal:

```
100 DEF FNA(A) = A + FNB(X,Y)
110 DEF FNB(X,Y) = X/Y + FNA(A)
```

The following function-summary program solves the polynomial

$$AX^2 + BX + C = 0$$

$$X = \frac{-B \pm \sqrt{B^2 - 4AC}}{2A}$$

In our program we must check to ensure that the value under the radical $(B^2 - 4AC)$ is not negative (roots are imaginary) and that $A$ does not equal zero (division by zero is impossible).

```
100 REM SOLVE A*X↑2 + B*X + C = 0 FOR X
110 REM                    USING QUADRATIC EQUATION
120 DEF FNX(A,B,C) = (-B + SQR(B↑2-4*A*C))/(2*A)
130 DEF FNY(A,B,C) = (-B - SQR(B↑2-4*A*C))/(2*A)
140 DEF FNZ(A,B,C) = B↑2 - 4*A*C
150 READ I,J,K
153 PRINT "A =" I; "B =" J; "C =" K
155 IF I=0 THEN 260
160 IF FNZ(I,J,K) < 0 THEN 230
170 PRINT "FIRST VALUE OF X IS" FNX(I,J,K)
180 PRINT "SECOND VALUE OF X IS" FNY(I,J,K)
190 PRINT
200 PRINT
210 PRINT
220 GOTO 150
230 PRINT "THESE ROOTS ARE IMAGINARY"
240 PRINT
250 GOTO 150
260 PRINT "IMPOSSIBLE"
265 GOTO 150
270 DATA 1.5, 5, 3
280 DATA 3, 6, 3
290 DATA 10, 7, 2
300 END
RUNNH
```

```
A =  1.5      B =  5      C =  3
FIRST VALUE OF X IS -.78475
SECOND VALUE OF X IS -2.54858



A =  3       B =  6       C =  3
FIRST VALUE OF X IS -1
SECOND VALUE OF X IS -1



A = 1Ø       B =  7       C =  2
THESE ROOTS ARE IMAGINARY

OUT OF DATA LINE 15Ø
```

### EXERCISES

1.  Enter and run the programs shown in *Utility Functions*, pages 60—61, to be sure you understand random number generation on your system.

2.  Reprogram the multiplication problem (exercises 4 and 5, page 56) to give the student his multiplication problems *randomly*. Select random multipliers and multiplicands in the range 2 through 12. After giving the student fifty problems, print VERY GOOD for up to three errors, GOOD for four through seven errors, or generate fifty more problems if more than seven errors are made.

§ 1.3    3.  Using only the addition, subtraction, exponentiation, and comparison operations, calculate and print the square root of 93 to the nearest one-thousandth.

    (Set some variable = 9—the square root of 93 is between 9 and 10. Repeatedly add .1 to the variable until you find the largest 1-decimal-digit number less than $\sqrt{93}$. The variable is tested by squaring it after each loop.

    Next, increment the second decimal digit, and the third and fourth, until you have found the largest 4-decimal-digit number less than $\sqrt{93}$. Use the rounding technique shown in *Arithmetic Functions*, page 59, to round the result to the nearest thousandth.

    A second variable should be set up as a counter to record the total number of loops required to perform the same operation as the SQR function.)

    The algorithm for solving this problem is discussed and flowcharted in example 1.3 of the Gear text.

    In the same program use the BASIC function SQR to verify your answer. (A possible solution is given in appendix B.)

4.  Write a program that calculates the average of the absolute values of a set of numbers and then the absolute value of the average of the same numbers. Ask the program's user how many numbers he wants to enter. Use the INPUT statement to enter the data.

5.  Define a function (FNC) to convert inches to centimeters. [Convert a value I (inches) to centimeters by calculating 2.54∗I.] Ask the program's user to enter three digits representing the length, width, and height of a box in inches. Using your FNC, print the length, width, and height in centimeters. Print the area of the base of the box in square centimeters. Print the volume of the box in cubic centimeters.

6.  Define a function (FNR) to convert degrees to radians (R = D∗3.14159265/180). Use FNR to print the sine, cosine, and tangent of any angle entered (in degrees) by the program's user. Be sure the angle falls between 0 and 90 degrees.

## FOOTNOTES AND REFERENCES

1   Gear, section 8.1, "Critical Paths."
2   Gear, section 3.7, "Built-in Functions."

Frequently, a program uses the same group of statements (a *subroutine*) in several places.[1] Rather than duplicate the subroutine everywhere it is needed, you can type it into one area of your program and use the statement GOSUB to call it whenever you want to.

GOSUB, like GOTO, causes a branch to the statement number indicated. When a GOSUB is used, however, the program saves the address of the instruction following the GOSUB, so that when the subroutine has been executed, control can return to the correct point in the main program. The RETURN statement marks the end of execution of the subroutine. It is actually a branch back to the saved address in the main program.

```
    GOSUB statement-nn
        .
        .
        .
    GOSUB statement-nn
        .
        .
        .
nn  REM BEGIN SUBROUTINE
        .
        .
    RETURN
```

**SAMPLE PROGRAM**

Consider, for example, the design of a simplified payroll program, WAGES. The program reads DATA statements containing the employee number, the employee's hourly wage, and the hours he worked on each day of the week, Sunday through Saturday.

    DATA 1234,3.00,0,8,8,6,8.5,10,3

indicates that employee 1234 earns $3.00 per hour. He worked eight hours on Monday and Tuesday, six hours on Wednesday, eight and one-half on Thursday, ten on Friday, and three on Saturday.

The program must print the hours worked and the dollars earned by the employee on each day of the week, and the total hours

Chapter

# 8

# Subroutines

worked and dollars earned for the week. The company pays double time for work on Sunday and time-and-a-half for work on Saturday. If an employee works more than eight hours on any weekday, he gets time-and-a-half for his overtime.

Following is a skeleton flowchart of the logic of the program.

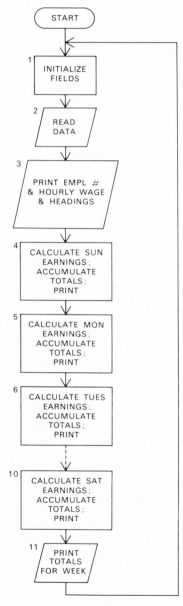

FIGURE 8–1   WAGES—Skeleton Flowchart

Notice that the logic for boxes 5–9 (Mon.–Fri.) is almost identical. Instead of coding the logic five times, it is coded once, as a subroutine, at the end of the program (lines 340–420) and is called by GOSUB statements (lines 130, 160, 190, 220, and 250).

## WAGES

```
10   LET H=Ø
20   LET E2=Ø
30   READ N,W,D1,D2,D3,D4,D5,D6,D7
40   PRINT "ENPLOYEE" N; "HOURLY WAGE" W
50   PRINT "DAY", "HOURS", "DOLLARS"
60   REM SUNDAY EARNINGS
70   LET E1=2*D1*W
80   LET H=H+D1
90   LET E2=E2+E1
100  PRINT "SUN", D1, E1
110  LET X=D2
120  LET D$="MON"
130  GOSUB 34Ø
140  LET X=D3
150  LET D$="TUES"
160  GOSUB 34Ø
170  LET X=D4
180  LET D$="WED"
190  GOSUB 34Ø
200  LET X=D5
210  LET D$="THURS"
220  GOSUB 34Ø
230  LET X=D6
240  LET D$="FRI"
250  GOSUB 34Ø
260  REM SATURDAY EARNINGS
270  LET E1=1.5*D7*W
280  LET H=H+D7
290  LET E2=E2+E1
300  PRINT "SAT", D7, E1
310  REM TOTAL EARNINGS
320  PRINT "TOTAL", H, E2
325  PRINT
330  GOTO 10
340  REM WEEKDAY EARNINGS - SUBROUTINE
350  IF X>8 THEN 38Ø
360  LET E1=X*W
370  GOTO 39Ø
380  LET E1=8*W + 1.5*W*(X-8)
390  LET H=H+X
400  LET E2=E2+E1
410  PRINT D$,X,E1
420  RETURN
500  DATA 1234, 3.ØØ, Ø, 8, 8, 6, 8.5, 1Ø, 3
510  DATA 1239, 3.1, 2, 8, 8, 8, 1Ø.5, Ø, 7
520  DATA 1333, 3.8Ø, Ø, 8, 8, 8, 8, 8, Ø
700  END
RUNNH
```

Initialize fields used to accumulate total hours and earnings for week. Employee number, hourly wage, 7 hours-worked figures.

Calculate earnings for Sunday. Accumulate hours for week. Accumulate earnings for week.

Prepare fields to be used by subroutine.

Process next employee.

Regular pay.

Overtime pay.

```
EMPLOYEE 1234        HOURLY WAGE 3
DAY                  HOURS               DOLLARS
SUN                  Ø                   Ø
MON                  8                   24
TUES                 8                   24
WED                  6                   18
THURS                8.5                 26.25
FRI                  1Ø                  33
SAT                  3                   13.5
TOTAL                43.5                138.75

EMPLOYEE 1239        HOURLY WAGE 3.1
DAY                  HOURS               DOLLARS
SUN                  2                   12.4
MON                  8                   24.8
TUES                 8                   24.8
WED                  8                   24.8
THURS                1Ø.5                36.425
FRI                  Ø                   Ø
SAT                  7                   32.55
TOTAL                43.5                155.775

EMPLOYEE 1333        HOURLY WAGE 3.8
DAY                  HOURS               DOLLARS
SUN                  Ø                   Ø
MON                  8                   3Ø.4
TUES                 8                   3Ø.4
WED                  8                   3Ø.4
THURS                8                   3Ø.4
FRI                  8                   3Ø.4
SAT                  Ø                   Ø
TOTAL                4Ø                  152.

OUT OF DATA   IN LINE 3Ø
```

## MULTIPLE SUBROUTINES

A program can have as many subroutines as needed, but each must end with a RETURN statement. In our WAGES program, the statements to accumulate total hours and total earnings and the statement to print the day's hours and earnings are coded three times (80–100, 280–300, and 390–410). These statements could be coded once, as a subroutine.

```
43Ø REM ACCUMULATE AND PRINT - SUBROUTINE
44Ø LET H=H+X
45Ø LET E2=E2+E1
46Ø PRINT D$, X, E1
47Ø RETURN
```

The Sunday coding would have to set up the variables X and D$ before calling the subroutine. Statements 80–100 would be replaced by the following:

```
8Ø  LET  X=D1
9Ø  LET  D$="SUN"
1ØØ  GOSUB  43Ø
```

Statements 280–300 would be changed similarly. Statements 390–410 would be replaced by the single statement:

```
39Ø  GOSUB  43Ø
```

### Nested Subroutines

With this change of statement 390, our new subroutine becomes a *nested subroutine*, because the first subroutine calls it. Subroutines may call other subroutines, but a subroutine may not call itself.

This change illustrates the use of nested subroutines, but it does not shorten the program or make it easier to follow. Therefore the original coding is a better solution to the problem. Did you notice another, simpler way to avoid coding the accumulations and printing three times? The Sunday and Saturday routines could set up the variables X and D$ and then GOSUB 39Ø. They would branch to the *end* of the weekday earnings subroutine, borrowing only a few statements of the subroutine. A second subroutine is not needed. This change illustrates the fact that, in BASIC, you can enter a subroutine at any point; but, again, in this case the change does not shorten or clarify the program.

### Modularized Programs

When you are tempted to use a subroutine, consider whether it will make the program easier or more difficult to follow. Sometimes it is wise to make a subroutine of logic that is needed only once in your program. For example, in the WAGES program we could have coded three subroutines: one for weekday earnings, one for Sunday earnings, and one for Saturday earnings. This would make the main body of the program very straightforward and easy to follow. It would be a series of GOSUBs and a routine to calculate the totals. Anyone reading the program could look at the subroutines at the end to see the calculations for each day of the week.

Extensive use of subroutines to clarify the program logic is called *modularizing* the program. This technique is often used in very large and complex programs to make the program easier to follow and to debug. A complex payroll program, for example, is a series of tests for special conditions with unique calculations for each condition. Is the employee salaried or hourly? Is he in the pension plan? Does he pay for health insurance? The main body of such a program might be a series of tests and branches to subroutines. Sometimes the various subroutines are coded and debugged by different programmers.

### Nesting Limit

When subroutines are nested, more than one return address must be saved, and they must be kept in sequence. Each BASIC system has some limit to the number of nested subroutines that can be coded (up to the number of current return addresses that can be saved). Normally this limit is far beyond your needs, so you don't have to worry about it; but if you're curious, you can test your system with a program such as the following.

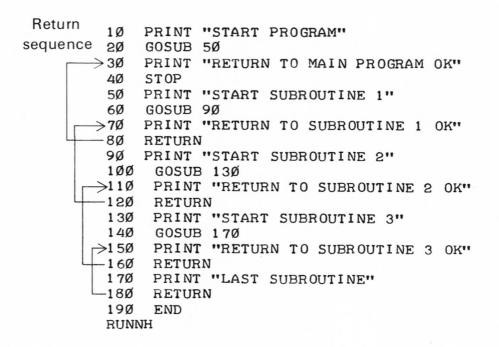

Return
sequence

```
10   PRINT "START PROGRAM"
20   GOSUB 50
30   PRINT "RETURN TO MAIN PROGRAM OK"
40   STOP
50   PRINT "START SUBROUTINE 1"
60   GOSUB 90
70   PRINT "RETURN TO SUBROUTINE 1  OK"
80   RETURN
90   PRINT "START SUBROUTINE 2"
100   GOSUB 130
110   PRINT "RETURN TO SUBROUTINE 2  OK"
120   RETURN
130   PRINT "START SUBROUTINE 3"
140   GOSUB 170
150   PRINT "RETURN TO SUBROUTINE 3  OK"
160   RETURN
170   PRINT "LAST SUBROUTINE"
180   RETURN
190   END
RUNNH
```

```
START PROGRAM
START SUBROUTINE 1
START SUBROUTINE 2
START SUBROUTINE 3
LAST SUBROUTINE
RETURN TO SUBROUTINE 3 OK
RETURN TO SUBROUTINE 2 OK
RETURN TO SUBROUTINE 1 OK
RETURN TO MAIN PROGRAM OK

DONE
```

Study this program to be sure that you understand the sequence of execution when subroutines are nested.

## MULTIPLE RETURNS

A subroutine must have at least one RETURN, although it can have more than one. The following subroutine calculates an employee's Social Security (FICA) payment (F). S is the employee's monthly salary and Y is the year-to-date salary that has been paid to him. FICA payments (5.2%) are deducted from only the first $7800 of the year's pay. The subroutine must determine if the employee has already earned $7800, if he will reach $7800 this pay period, or if he will remain below $7800. It has three RETURNS, one after each of the three possible methods of calculating FICA.

```
500 REM FICA SUBROUTINE
510 IF Y >= 7800 THEN 560
520 IF Y+S >= 7800 THEN 590
530 REM CALCULATE FICA ON FULL SALARY
540 LET F = .025*S
550 RETURN
560 REM YEAR'S FICA HAS ALREADY BEEN PAID
570 LET F=0
580 RETURN
590 REM FINISH OFF FICA FOR YEAR
600 LET F = .052*(7800-Y)
610 RETURN
```

Note that any two of the RETURNs could be replaced by a branch to (GOTO) the third.

## PLACEMENT OF SUBROUTINES

You can place subroutines anywhere in your program, but be sure it is not possible for a subroutine to be executed without being called by a GOSUB. If the program falls into a subroutine instead of being sent there by a GOSUB, it won't know what to do when it reaches the RETURN statement. Statement 330 in our WAGES program (a branch back to the beginning of the program) prevents this from happening.

Because of this potential problem, subroutines are usually placed near the end of the program. The statement preceding the subroutines is commonly a branch back into the main program or, if processing is complete, a STOP statement.

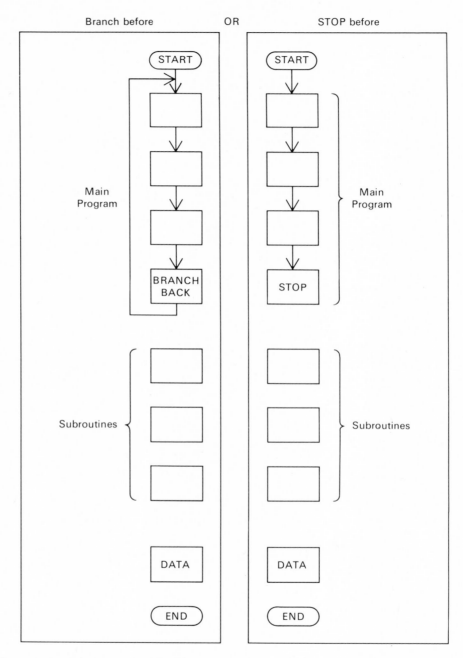

FIGURE 8–2   Placement of Subroutines

**EXERCISES**

1.  A driver has compiled the following data on the gas mileage of his car:

    ● Using low-grade gasoline (28.9¢ per gallon), he drove 182 miles on 10.6 gallons
    ● Using medium-grade gas (32.9¢), he drove 98 miles on 5.5 gallons
    ● Using high-grade gas (37.9¢), he drove 198 miles on 10 gallons

    Enter a program to tell him how many cents it costs him to drive one mile using each of the three grades of gasoline.

    (Cents per mile = cost times gallons-used/miles-driven.)

    In the main program print the headings GRADE and COST PER MILE; use LET statements to assign the data values; print the grade for which a calculation is about to be made; then branch to a subroutine that calculates and prints the cost per mile. Reassign the data values and call the subroutine twice more.

2.  Write a program to calculate and print the number of days, hours, minutes, and seconds in each month of the year.
    *a.*  Print headings:  MONTHS  DAYS  HOURS  MINUTES  SECONDS
    *b.*  Code thirteen routines that set up a numerical variable with the correct number of days for that month and a string variable with the correct abbreviation for that month (JAN, FEB, FEB—LEAP, MAR, . . . DEC).
    *c.*  Let each routine branch to a subroutine that does the actual calculation and printing.

**FOOTNOTES AND REFERENCES**

1   Gear, section 5.4, "Procedures—Subroutines."

## ARRAY TERMINOLOGY

Any variables mentioned up to this point in the book have been simple variables. This chapter describes the handling of *subscripted variables* (such as $X_a$ or $X_{a,b}$) used to reference rows and/or columns of numbers.[1]

Numerical arrays with only one dimension are referenced by subscripted variables such as $X_a$, and are called *lists* or *vectors*. Two-dimensional arrays, referenced by variables such as $X_{a,b}$, are called *matrices* or *tables*. Arrays containing more than two dimensions are not permitted in most BASIC systems.

Individual members in an array are called *elements* and are identified by subscripts. $A_5$ is the fifth element of vector A. $B_{2,3}$ refers to the element in the second row, third column of matrix B.

Vector A : $A_1$ $A_2$ $A_3$ $A_4$ $A_5$ $A_6$

Matrix B : 

$$
\begin{array}{cccc}
B_{1,1} & B_{1,2} & B_{1,3} & B_{1,4} \\
B_{2,1} & B_{2,2} & B_{2,3} & B_{2,4} \\
B_{3,1} & B_{3,2} & B_{3,3} & B_{3,4}
\end{array}
$$

Because subscripts cannot be entered on our terminals, BASIC permits them to be enclosed in parentheses.

| Arithmetic Representation | BASIC Notation |
|---|---|
| $X_3$ | X(3) |
| $Y_{a,b}$ | Y(A,B) |
| $Z_{a+b/2}$ | Z(A+B/2) |

As you can see from these examples, subscripts can be mathematical expressions. X(3) refers to the third element in vector X. To locate the elements referenced by the second and third examples, BASIC finds the values of the expressions in parentheses. If $A=4$ and $B=8$, then Y(A,B) refers to the eighth element in the fourth row of matrix Y. If the subscript is not an integer, BASIC ignores the nonintegral part. For example, if $A=2$ and $B=11$, then Z(A+B/2) refers to the seventh entry in vector Z.

## NAMING ARRAYS

In most BASIC systems, array names are limited to the alphabetic characters A through Z (twenty-six total arrays per program). An array and a simple variable referenced in the same program can have the same name, but this is not a good programming practice. Ambiguity can be avoided by including the digit permitted as a second character in simple variable names (for example, A1, B1 instead of A, B if arrays named A and B are included in the same program).

## DEFINING ARRAY DIMENSIONS

If you have no more than ten entries in a vector or no more than ten rows and ten columns in a matrix, you don't have to define your array formally. When BASIC encounters the subscripted variable X(A) in your program, it automatically reserves ten consecutive fields in memory for vector X. If it encounters the subscripted variable Y(A,B), it reserves 100 consecutive fields.

### The DIM Statement

If you require more fields than those reserved automatically, you must use the dimension statement (DIM) to tell BASIC how much memory you need. The dimension statement has the following format:

    DIM array—1(size),array—2(size), . . . , array—n(size)

Example:

## 1Ø DIM A(5Ø), B(3,15), C(12), X(15,5)

The *size* (number of elements) is one integer for a vector and two integers for a matrix (the number of rows followed by the number of columns). One dimension statement can define any number of arrays within the limit of the input line and can appear anywhere in your program.

### Array Values

Array elements, like simple variables, don't have values until you assign them. You can use LET, INPUT, or READ statements (or special matrix statements described later in this chapter) to load values into your array.

The following RAIN2 program, like the RAIN1 example in chapter 5, calculates the average monthly rainfall for one year. Note that string data can be loaded into a vector [M$(12) in statement 10]. In most BASIC systems, however, string data cannot be loaded into a *matrix*. String vector values are discussed further in chapter 10.

The I loop (statements 20—40) loads values into array M$. The J loop (statements 50—80) uses the data in array M$ and loads values into array R. The K loop (statements 100—120) totals the data in array R.

The RAIN3 program on page 81 reads rainfall data for up to thirty years and places it in a table. It prints the average rainfall for each year and then performs a *table lookup*. (The operator can enter a month and a year, and the

```
1Ø M$(12),R(12)
2Ø FOR I = 1 TO 12
3Ø READ M$(I)
4Ø NEXT I
5Ø FOR J = 1 TO 12
6Ø PRINT "ENTER RAINFALL FOR" M$(J)
7Ø INPUT R(J)
8Ø NEXT J
9Ø LET T=Ø
1ØØ FOR K = 1 TO 12
11Ø LET T = T + R(K)
12Ø NEXT K
13Ø PRINT "AVERAGE MONTHLY RAINFALL IS" T/12
14Ø DATA "JAN", "FEB", "MARCH", "APRIL", "MAY", "JUNE", "JULY"
15Ø DATA "AUG", "SEPT", "OCT", "NOV", "DEC"
16Ø END
RUNNH


ENTER RAINFALL FOR JAN
?1.2
ENTER RAINFALL FOR FEB
?.9
ENTER RAINFALL FOR MARCH
?.6
ENTER RAINFALL FOR APRIL
?.2
ENTER RAINFALL FOR MAY
?.5
ENTER RAINFALL FOR JUNE
?.8
ENTER RAINFALL FOR JULY
?.6
ENTER RAINFALL FOR AUG
?.9
ENTER RAINFALL FOR SEPT
?1.Ø
ENTER RAINFALL FOR OCT
?1.8
ENTER RAINFALL FOR NOV
?1.3
ENTER RAINFALL FOR DEC
?2.1
AVERAGE MONTHLY RAINFALL IS .991667
```

program will look up and print the amount of rainfall for that month.)

The program is shown first in flowchart form. To help you follow the program logic, program statement numbers are shown in the flowchart. Note the use of imbedded FOR—NEXT loops to step through the elements in the matrix. These and other matrix functions can be performed more simply, as will be shown in the next section.

If you have any difficulty following the logic of RAIN 3, you will appreciate the simplicity of the MAT statements that follow the program.

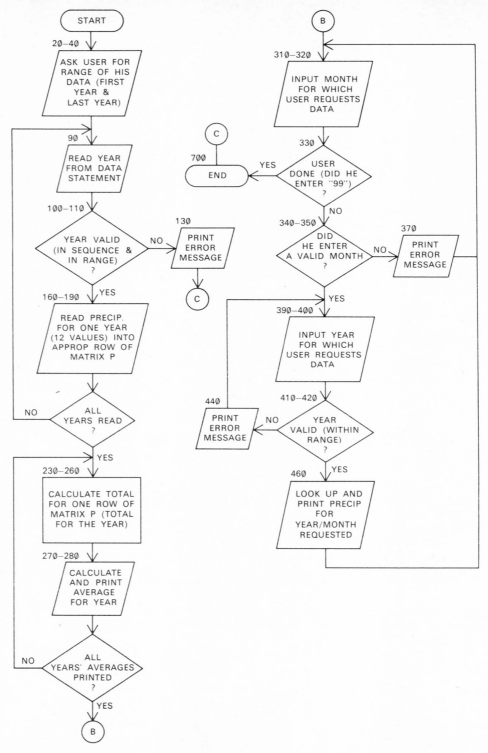

FIGURE 9-1    Flowchart for RAIN3 with Statement Numbers

```
10 DIM P(30,12)                                        Matrix P will contain the precipitation
                                                       for each month of each year.

20 PRINT "ENTER FIRST YEAR"
30 INPUT F
40 PRINT "ENTER LAST YEAR"
50 INPUT L
60 LET S = F-1                                         S = the previous year;
                                                       used for sequence
                                                       checking of years.
                                                       L - F + 1 = the total number
                                                                    of years.

70 FOR I = 1 TO L-F+1                                  Read year.
80 REM ROUTINE TO CHECK VALIDITY OF YEARS              Check to see that the
90 READ Y                                              year is in sequence.
100 IF Y <> S+1 THEN 130                               Check to see that the
                                                       year is in range.
110 IF Y > L THEN 130                                  Year is OK.
                                                       Year not OK.
120 GOTO 150                                           Terminate.
130 PRINT "WRONG SEQUENCE OR DATA OUT OF RANGE"        This year will be "previous
140 GOTO 700                                           year" next time through.
150 LET S=Y

160 REM LOAD VALUES INTO MATRIX P                      Fill one row of matrix
170 FOR J = 1 TO 12                                    P (one year's data).
180 READ P(I,J)                                        Go back to next year.
190 NEXT J
200 NEXT I
210 REM CALCULATE AVERAGES
```

```
220  FOR K = 1 TO L-F+1
230  LET T=0
240  FOR Q = 1 TO 12
250  LET T = T + P(K,Q)

260  NEXT Q

270  PRINT "AVERAGE MONTHLY RAINFALL FOR" F+K-1
280  PRINT T/12
190  NEXT K
300  REM EXAMPLE OF TABLE LOOKUP
310  PRINT "ENTER MONTH 1-12: OR 99 IF DONE"
320  INPUT M

330  IF M = 99 THEN 700

340  IF M < 1 THEN 370
350  IF M > 12 THEN 370
360  GOTO 390

370  PRINT "INVALID ENTRY"
380  GOTO 310
390  PRINT "ENTER YEAR" F "TO" L
400  INPUT Y2

410  IF Y2 < F THEN 440
420  IF Y2 > L THEN 440
```

For each year:
Start with total precipitation = 0.
For each month of each year:
add appropriate element to T (total for year).
Go back to get next month of this year.

F + K – 1 = the year.
Print average for the year.
Go back to get next year.

User inputs month for which he wants data.
If user input 99, he is done, so terminate.
Check to see that he input a valid month.
Month is OK; go to 390 for year.
Month not OK.
Let user try again.

User enters year for which he wants data.
Check to see that he input year within range.

```
430 GOTO 460                                        Year is OK; go to 460
                                                    to look up his answer.
440 PRINT "INVALID"                                 Year not OK.
450 GOTO 390                                        Let user try again.
460 PRINT "RAIN FOR" M "/" Y2 "IS" P(Y2-F+1,M)         Look up his answer.
                                                    (It is in row Y2 − F + 1,
                                                    column M.
470 GOTO 310                                        Return to get another
                                                                user request.

480 REM DATA CARDS CONTAIN YEAR FOLLOWED BY 12 VALUES
490 DATA 1961, 3.2, 2.7, 1.9, 1.6, .5, .6, .7, .9, 1.1, 1.1, 1.8, 1.9
500 DATA 1962, 2.1, 2.9, 1.5, 1.7, .2, .1, .4, .9, 1.5, 1.5, 1.8
510 DATA 1963, 1.8, 2.0, 1.3, 1.2, .9, .5, .3, 0, .4, .8, 1.2, 1.5
700 END
RUNNH

ENTER FIRST YEAR
?1961
ENTER LAST YEAR
?1963
AVERAGE MONTHLY RAINFALL FOR 1961
 1.5
AVERAGE MONTHLY RAINFALL FOR 1962
 1.275
AVERAGE MONTHLY RAINFALL FOR 1963
 .991667
```

```
ENTER MONTH 1-12: OR 99 IF DONE
?13
INVALID ENTRY
ENTER MONTH 1-12: OR 99 IF DONE
?12
ENTER YEAR 1961   TO 1963
?1961
RAIN FOR 12  / 1961   IS 1.9
ENTER MONTH 1-12: OR 99 IF DONE
?2
ENTER YEAR 1961   TO 1963
?1963
RAIN FOR 2  / 1963   IS 2
ENTER MONTH 1-12: OR 99 IF DONE
?99

DONE
```

## MATRIX MANIPULATION[2]

### The MAT Statements

All matrix functions could be programmed using subscripts with statements already covered. However, a special set of thirteen matrix statements allows you to shorten your BASIC program and simplify calculations. Each matrix statement begins with the word MAT. They are as follows:

| | |
|---|---|
| MAT READ X,Y,Z | Read data from DATA statements into previously dimensioned matrices in row sequence. |
| MAT INPUT X,Y | Input data into previously dimensioned matrices in row sequence. |
| MAT PRINT X | Print the elements of matrix X. |
| MAT Y = X | Set the elements of matrix Y equivalent to the corresponding elements of matrix X; X is not altered. |
| MAT Z = X + Y | Add the elements of matrix X to the corresponding elements of matrix Y; place the totals in matrix Z. |
| MAT Z = X − Y | Subtract the elements of matrix Y from the corresponding elements of matrix X; place the results in matrix Z. |
| MAT Z = X*Y | Multiply the elements of matrix X by the elements of matrix Y; place the products in matrix Z. |
| MAT Z = (V)*X | Multiply the elements of matrix X by the value V (scalar multiplication); V is a mathematical expression and must be enclosed in parentheses. |
| MAT Z = INV(X) | Invert matrix X; place the new version in matrix Z. X is not altered. |
| MAT Z = TRN(X) | Transpose matrix X; place the new version in matrix Z. X is not altered. |
| MAT X = ZER | Load zeros into all elements of matrix X. |
| MAT X = CON | Load ones into all elements of matrix X. (CON stands for constant). |
| MAT X = IDN | Set up matrix X as an "identity" matrix (diagonal elements = one; nondiagonal elements = zero). |

Detailed discussions of these operations can be found in any book on matrix algebra. The example program on the following pages, MATTER, may clear up initial questions you might have about the effect of certain MAT statements.

```
10  DIM X(3,3),Y(3,3),Z(3,3)
20  MAT READ X,Y
25  PRINT "MATRIX X"
30  MAT PRINT X;
35  PRINT
40  PRINT "MATRIX Y"
50  MAT PRINT Y;
60  MAT Z = X+Y
70  PRINT "MATRIX Z = X+Y"
80  MAT PRINT Z;
85  PRINT
90  MAT X = TRN(Z)
100 PRINT "NEW MATRIX X = Z TRANSPOSED"
110 MAT PRINT X;
115 PRINT
120 MAT Y = INV(X)
130 PRINT "NEW MATRIX Y = INVERSE OF X"
140 MAT PRINT Y
145 PRINT
150 MAT Z = X*Y
160 PRINT "NEW MATRIX Z = X*INVERSE OF X = IDN"
170 MAT PRINT Z
180 DATA 1,4,9,7,2,3,8,6,5
190 DATA 20,60,50,70,10,90,40,80,30
200 END
RUNNH
```

MATRIX X

| 1 | 4 | 9 |
|---|---|---|
| 7 | 2 | 3 |
| 8 | 6 | 5 |

MATRIX Y

| 2Ø | 6Ø | 5Ø |
|----|----|----|
| 7Ø | 1Ø | 9Ø |
| 4Ø | 8Ø | 3Ø |

MATRIX Z = X+Y

| 21 | 64 | 59 |
|----|----|----|
| 77 | 12 | 93 |
| 48 | 86 | 35 |

NEW MATRIX X = Z TRANSPOSED

| 21 | 77 | 48 |
|----|----|----|
| 64 | 12 | 86 |
| 59 | 93 | 35 |

NEW MATRIX Y = INVERSE OF X

| $-2.43829E-Ø2$ | $5.69191E-Ø3$ | $1.94535E-Ø2$ |
|----|----|----|
| $9.11864E-Ø3$ | $-6.74728E-Ø3$ | $4.Ø7347E-Ø3$ |
| $.Ø16873$ | $8.33355E-Ø3$ | $-1.5Ø454E-Ø2$ |

NEW MATRIX Z = X*INVERSE OF X = IDN

| $1.$ | $-5.96Ø46E-Ø8$ | $1.192Ø9E-Ø7$ |
|----|----|----|
| $Ø$ | $1.$ | $Ø$ |
| $-2.38419E-Ø7$ | $1.78814E-Ø7$ | $1.$ |

DONE

**Matrix Input/Output**

The MAT READ, MAT INPUT, and MAT PRINT instructions are used to read data into or type data from a matrix without referencing each element individually. Any number of matrices can be read or printed within the limits of the input line.

As shown in the MATTER program, the MAT READ statement fills a matrix, and the MAT PRINT statement prints it, in *row* (horizontal) sequence.

```
10  DIM X(2,3)
20  MAT READ X
30  MAT PRINT X;
40  DATA 1, 2, 3, -4, -5, -6
50  END
RUNNH
```

| 1 | 2 | 3 |
|---|---|---|
| -4 | -5 | -6 |

.

DONE

The values stored in this example would be referenced by the following subscripts:

$X(1,1) = 1$
$X(1,2) = 2$
$X(1,3) = 3$
$X(2,1) = -4$
$X(2,2) = -5$
$X(2,3) = -6$

MAT READ and MAT INPUT also let you redimension your matrix size at execution time (that is, make one or both of its dimensions, as previously defined, smaller). The forms used are:

MAT READ A(R,C)
MAT INPUT A(R,C)

where R is the new number of rows and C is the new number of columns. R and C are both mathematical expressions.

The following code could replace statements 10–200 of program RAIN3. Statement 70 fills matrix P and redimensions it so it has the correct number of rows for the data of this particular run. The MAT READ statement eliminates the need for the imbedded FOR–NEXT loops of RAIN3 statements 70 and 170 and makes the program easier to follow. If this change is made to RAIN3, the years, as well as the rainfall data, are read into the matrix. Statement 240 would have to be changed to

        240 FOR Q = 2 TO 13

to avoid adding the year into the average rainfall calculation. How would you alter RAIN3 statement 460 to accommodate this change?[3]

```
10  DIM P(30,13)
20  PRINT "ENTER FIRST YEAR"
30  INPUT F
40  PRINT "ENTER LAST YEAR"
50  INPUT L
60  IF L-F+1 > 30 THEN 160
70  MAT READ P(L-F+1, 13)
80  REM CHECK VALIDITY OF YEARS
90  LET S = F-1
100 FOR A = 1 TO L-F+1
110 IF P(A,1) <> S+1 THEN 160
120 LET S = P(A,1)
130 NEXT A
140 GOTO 210
150 REM ERROR ROUTINE FOR BAD DATA
160 PRINT "TOO MUCH DATA OR DATA OUT OF SEQUENCE OR RANGE"
170 GOTO 700
```

### Matrix Arithmetic

Matrices can be made equivalent, added, subtracted, or multiplied using the five arithmetic MAT statements:

        MAT Z = X           Equivalence
        MAT Z = X + Y       Addition
        MAT Z = X − Y       Subtraction
        MAT Z = X*Y         Multiplication
        MAT Z = (V)*X       Scalar Multiplication

Matrix dimensions must be "conformable" for all arithmetic operations. This means specifically:

- For addition and subtraction, the dimensions of the matrices to the right of the equal sign must be identical.

```
1Ø DIM X(12,15), Y(12,15), Z(15,15)
 •
 •
 •
6Ø MAT Z = X + Y
```

• For multiplication, at least the two "inner" elements must be equal.

```
1Ø DIM X(1Ø,4), Y(4,12), Z(2Ø,2Ø)
 •
 •
 •
6Ø MAT Z = X*Y
```

produces a 10 by 12 matrix.

In any of the arithmetic MAT statements, the result matrix can be larger than the actual result. (Z is larger than 12 by 15 in the addition example and larger than 10 by 12 in the multiplication example.) When this is the case, the result matrix is redimensioned to the appropriate size when the arithmetic MAT statement is executed.

The same matrix can appear on both sides of the MAT equation in addition, subtraction, and scalar multiplication. Thus, the following statements are legal, provided the matrices are properly dimensioned.

```
1ØØ MAT X = X+Y
11Ø MAT X = (.ØØ1)*X
12Ø MAT X = X-Y
```

Only one arithmetic operation is allowed per statement.

Illegal :

```
1ØØ MAT X = X + Y - Z
```

This statement would have to be reprogrammed as two separate operations.

### Matrix Transposition

MAT READ and MAT INPUT accept data in row sequence. MAT TRN has the effect of resequencing a matrix in column, or vertical, order. See the MATTER program for an example. The dimensions of your new matrix must be such that its column-row values equal the row-column values of the old matrix.

```
1Ø DIM X(6,3),Y(3,6)
 •
 •
 •
6Ø MAT Y = TRN(X)
```

Transposition in place does not work on most systems. The same matrix cannot appear on both sides of a transposition statement.

### Initializing Matrices

The MAT statements ZER, CON, and IDN allow you to load specific values into the elements of a matrix without having to READ or INPUT them. All three can be used to redimension a matrix using the same format as MAT READ.

        MAT Z = ZER(R,C)
        MAT Z = CON(R,C)
        MAT Z = IDN(R,C)

**Initializing to Zero**   The statement

        MAT Z = ZER

loads zeros into every element of matrix Z.

**Initializing to One**   The statement

        MAT W = CON

loads a one into each element of matrix W.

**The Identity Matrix**   The IDN statement creates an identity matrix; that is, a matrix whose diagonal elements equal one and whose nondiagonal elements equal zero.

```
1Ø  MAT X = IDN(3,3)
2Ø  MAT PRINT X;
3Ø  END
RUNNH


    1         Ø         Ø

    Ø         1         Ø

    Ø         Ø         1


DONE
```

Note that statement 10 redimensions matrix X. Since there is no DIM statement defining X, it would be assumed to be 10 by 10 if the dimensions (3,3) were not included.

If your matrix is not dimensioned to be square—for example,

DIM X(15,15) —you will receive a dimension error message if you try to use it in an IDN statement.

### Matrix Inversion

The statement

MAT Z = INV(Y)

calculates the inverse of matrix Y $\left( \dfrac{1}{Y} \text{ or } Y^{-1} \right)$ . Matrix inversion is the most powerful of the BASIC matrix operations, accomplishing in a single statement what would be a mammoth task using regular BASIC features. Its main use is in solving simultaneous linear equations.[4] For example, we can organize the equations

$$3X_1 + X_2 - 2X_3 = 20$$
$$-2X_1 + 2X_2 + 5X_3 = -2$$
$$4X_2 + X_3 = 26$$

so that Y is the matrix of coefficients, X is the column vector of unknown quantities, and Z is the column vector of values to the right of the equal sign.

$$\text{Matrix } Y = \begin{matrix} 3 & 1 & -2 \\ -2 & 2 & 5 \\ 0 & 4 & 1 \end{matrix}$$

$$\text{Vector } X = \begin{matrix} X_1 \\ X_2 \\ X_3 \end{matrix}$$

$$\text{Vector } Z = \begin{matrix} 20 \\ -2 \\ 26 \end{matrix}$$

Our set of equations can, therefore, be reduced to the formula

YX = Z

or, solving for the unknown quantities,

X = Z/Y

or X = Y$^{-1}$Z

where Y$^{-1}$ is the inverse of the matrix Y.

Our problem can be solved quite simply, now, by inverting the matrix Y and multiplying the result by Z. Note that the MAT multiplication statement can be applied to the latter operation; the vector Z is merely treated as a special matrix having a single column. Statement 10 is optional in the following program, LINEAR, but is included for clarity.

```
10 DIM Y(3,3), U(3,3), X(3), Z(3)
20 MAT READ Y,Z
30 MAT U = INV(Y)
40 MAT X = U*Z
50 MAT PRINT X
60 DATA 3, 1, -2
70 DATA -2, 2, 5
80 DATA 0, 4, 1
90 DATA 20, -2, 26
100 END
RUNNH
```

3.

7

-2.


DONE


The solution of our equations is

$X_1 = 3$
$X_2 = 7$
$X_3 = -2$


**EXERCISES**

1.  Modify the multiplication testing program (exercise 2 of chapter 7) to guarantee that no problem is posed more than once (if answered correctly) in a set of fifty problems. Use an array of "switches," all of which are OFF (zero) before you begin to test the student. Turn the appropriate switch ON (one) when the student has correctly answered a problem. [Multiplying $7 \times 3$ correctly turns on element (7,3) of the switch table.] Leave the switch off if he makes a mistake. Before you give him a problem, test to be sure that the switch for that problem is still OFF.

In this exercise, reversing the multiplier and multiplicand creates a new problem ($7 \times 3$ and $3 \times 7$ are different problems and both should be posed). If the test is restarted because the student has made too many errors, reset all switches OFF.

2. Write a program to solve the following set of equations:

$$3A + 2B + C - 5D = 3$$
$$A + B + C + 2D = 17$$
$$5A - 10B + C/2 - 2D = 28$$
$$10A + 5C = 0$$

3. Students in a data-processing course have received seven grades during the semester. Flowchart and enter a program to assign final grades. The program should read the following DATA statements:

```
DATA    CANTOR,99,87,A,B,B,A,A
DATA    MEADOWS,83,79,C,C,C,B,B
DATA    TELLER,62,41,D,D,F,F,F
DATA    RUDERMAN,99,100,A,A,A,A,A
DATA    HUMPHRY,95,87,B,A,A,A,A
DATA    HOUDE,88,90,C,C,B,B,A
```

The fields in the DATA statements are as follows:
1    The student's name
2    Midterm exam grade; 20% of the final grade
3    Final exam grade; 30% of the final grade
4–8    Grades on each of five programs; each counts 10% toward the final grade. Convert the alphabetic grades to the following numerical equivalents:
   A   97
   B   91
   C   84
   D   75
   F   65

Print the student's name in print position 1, his final numerical average in position 16, and his final alphabetic grade in position 25. Convert the final numerical average to an alphabetic grade according to the following ranges:

   A   94 or greater
   B   88 through 93
   C   80 through 87
   D   70 through 79
   F   less than 70

4.  There are six baseball teams in the American League western division. Each has been assigned a team number, from one through six.

(1)  California Angels
(2)  Chicago White Sox
(3)  Kansas City Royals
(4)  Minnesota Twins
(5)  Oakland Athletics
(6)  Texas Rangers

Write a program that will read DATA statements containing information about a single baseball game in the following format:

team number,score,team number,score

Example:

DATA 5,9,3,3

represents a game in which Oakland defeated Kansas City 9–3.
As you read the data, accumulate—

● The number of games won by each team
● and the number of runs scored by each team—

against each of its opponents.

The statement

DATA 9,9,9,9

will indicate the end of data.
Keep the totals in two-dimensional arrays so that, after reading all the data, your program can access information about the number of games played, the number of wins, and the runs scored for each *pair* of teams.

*a.*  Print the total number of wins and losses and the average number of runs per game for each team.
*b.*  Allow the program's user to enter two team numbers. Print the number of wins each team has over the other, and the average number of runs each team has scored in games against the other.

(One possible solution is given in appendix B.)
*Note:* Because this program READs data instead of INPUTing it, the data can be stored with the program. When more data is available, it can be added to the program; previous data need not be reentered.

### FOOTNOTES AND REFERENCES

1   Gear, section 3.6, "Arrays."
2   Gear, section 3.6.1, "Higher Dimensional Arrays."
3   Statement 460 would have to print $P(Y2 - F + 1, M + 1)$ instead of $P(Y2 - F + 1, M)$.
4   Compare this discussion with the more complex handling of linear equations in Gear, section 9.4, "Linear Equations—Gauss Elimination."

BASIC allows you to input, output, store, and compare alphamerical and special characters, as well as numbers.[1] A sequence of these characters is called a *string* and the name identifying such a sequence is a *string variable*.

When strings were first introduced into BASIC, their length was limited to fifteen characters. Today the permissible length varies; the length of the input line is a frequently quoted limit. You can test the limits of your particular BASIC system by writing a short program to INPUT and PRINT strings of varying lengths.

## NAMING STRING VARIABLES

A dollar sign ($) is appended to a regular variable name to form a string-variable name. The conservative and safest approach here is to name your strings using only an alphabetic character followed by the dollar sign.

A$, B$, . . .Z$

Many systems are getting away from this early BASIC restriction and allow a digit as the second character of a string-variable name just as with numerical-variable names (A0$, A1$, . . .Z9$). The shorter form restriction, however, is still widespread.

## DIMENSIONING STRINGS

Arrays can contain string data also. String arrays are named using the same conventions as nonsubscripted string-variable names.

DIM A$(15),B$(12)

Here again, conservative programming would limit string-array names to an alphabetic character followed by a dollar sign and would also limit arrays to one dimension. The tendency is toward a two-dimensional array capability, but this is not yet a widely implemented feature. There are obvious advantages in being able to set up string tables and this capability should soon become commonplace. For example, the dimension statement

Chapter

# 10

# STRING MANIPULATION

```
10 DIM E$(12,5)
```

might be used to provide a primary reference to twelve employee names and a secondary reference to five subcategories such as city of birth, state of birth, sex, marital status, and age.

String-array dimensions and normal-array dimensions can be defined in the same DIM statement.

```
10 DIM E$(12), X(15), J$(33), Y(12,12)
```

As with numerical arrays, if no subscript exceeds ten, the DIM statement isn't necessary.[2]

## STRING INPUT

### Direct Assignment

The LET statement can be used to load a string constant (string data enclosed in quotation marks) into a string variable, or to set one string variable equal to another.

```
20 LET P$(1) = "STRING"
30 LET P$(2) = P$(1)
40 LET M$ = P$(2)
50 PRINT P$(1); TAB(20); M$
60 PRINT TAB(12); P$(2)
70 END
RUNNH
```

STRING                          STRING
               STRING

In most systems, LET is optional (see chapter 4) and statements 20 through 40 can be written as:

```
20 P$(1) = "STRING"
30 P$(2) = P$(1)
40 M$ = P$(2)
```

### READ and INPUT Statements

Both READ and INPUT can be used to enter combinations of string and numerical data. Input strings are frequently enclosed in quotation marks to avoid confusion between them and numbers.

Many systems have dropped the requirement for using quotation marks around data entered in response to the INPUT statement or entered in DATA statements (with the exception of strings containing commas and leading or trailing blanks). This is sensible because the $ in the variable name tells BASIC to expect string input for that variable. In any case, you won't go wrong if quotation marks are included.

```
1Ø READ N$, C$, S$, G$, A, M$
    •
    •
    •
1ØØ DATA "BROWN, MARY", OAKLAND, "CA  ", FEMALE, 3Ø, M
```

The data values for N$ and S$ in this example require quotation marks because a comma is included in the first case and trailing blanks in the second.

Again, to really understand your system, experiment!

### RESTORE Statement

The RESTORE statement can be used to reset the next READ statement to the first element of the first DATA statement, as is done with numerical input data. RESTORE makes no distinction between numerical and string information.

### STRING OUTPUT

As we've seen in earlier chapters, string constants used in PRINT statements must be enclosed in quotation marks. As with READ and INPUT, the PRINT instruction can reference a combination of string and numerical variables. A semicolon following a string designation in a PRINT statement causes any variable data following that string to be appended to it in the typed output.

```
1Ø  READ A, A$, B$, B, C$
2Ø  PRINT B$; C$; A
3Ø  PRINT A$; C$; B
4Ø  DATA 123•Ø7, "FINAL ", "SUB"
5Ø  DATA 517•26, "TOTAL IS  "
6Ø  END
RUNNH


SUBTOTAL IS   123•Ø7
FINAL TOTAL IS   517•26

DONE
```

The semicolon following B$ in statement 20 causes SUBTOTAL to be printed as one word. A space was included in the string "FINAL" in statement 40 so that FINAL TOTAL would not be printed as one word.

## COMPARING STRINGS

An attempt to perform an arithmetic operation on string variables or constants causes an error message to be issued. You can, however, *compare* strings using IF–THEN and the relational operators (see chapters 4 and 7).

If strings of different length are compared, the shorter string is compared with the corresponding segment (left-justified) of the longer string; if the segments compare equally, the short string is considered to be less than the long string (in effect, the short string is padded with blanks, which compare less than any other character). Thus HAT is considered to be less than HATE, but HAY is greater than HATE.

Only one string variable or constant can appear on each side of the relational operator.

```
100 IF N$ = "ROSIE" THEN 200
110 IF N$ <> "ROSIE" THEN 300
120 IF X$ <= Y$ THEN 360
```

The sequence used to compare characters in BASIC is shown in the following table, starting with the highest.[3]

TABLE 1    Sequence for Comparing BASIC Characters

High

| I | II | III | IV | V |
|---|----|-----|----|----|
| ← | @ | : | + | % |
| ↑ | ? | 9 to 0 | * | $ |
| ] | > | / | ) | # |
| \ | = | . | ( | '' |
| [ | < | – | ' | ! |
| Z to A | ; | , | & | (blank) |

Low

Thus T is greater than ? which is greater than 5 which is greater than !.

The NAMSRT program that follows uses the string array and compares features to alphabetize a list of twelve names.

```
1Ø DIM NS(12)
2Ø FOR I = 1 TO 12
3Ø READ NS(I)
4Ø NEXT I
5Ø FOR K = 1 TO 11
6Ø FOR J = 1 TO 11
7Ø LET AS = NS(J)
8Ø LET BS = NS(J+1)
9Ø IF AS <= BS THEN 12Ø
1ØØ LET NS(J) = BS
11Ø LET NS(J+1) = AS
12Ø NEXT J
13Ø NEXT K
14Ø FOR L = 1 TO 12
15Ø PRINT NS(L),
16Ø NEXT L
17Ø DATA "JUDY", "KATHY", "DEBORAH", "LINDA"
18Ø DATA "BARBARA", "RENATE", "TAMARA", "CATHY"
19Ø DATA "EILEEN", "NANCY", "JUDITH", "AMY"
2ØØ END
RUNNH
```

| AMY | BARBARA | CATHY | DEBORAH | EILEEN |
|-----|---------|-------|---------|--------|
| JUDITH | JUDY | KATHY | LINDA | NANCY |
| RENATE | TAMARA | | | |

**EXERCISES**

1. Modify the NAMSRT program to sort into descending rather than ascending sequence.

2. Write a program that accepts twentieth-century dates in numerical notation and prints them written out in full.

   Example:

   User enters 11,Ø4,44
   Program prints NOVEMBER 4, 1944

3. Write a program that can be used to encode and decode short messages.
   *a.* READ (from a DATA statement)
   - The twenty-six letters of the alphabet
   - The digits 0—9
   - A blank, a comma, and a period into a 39-element list (the "code array").

b.  Ask the program's user to enter his message. The message should not be more than thirty characters long and should be terminated by an asterisk. The characters must be separated by commas; if commas or blanks are to be included as part of the message, they must be enclosed in quotation marks. Asterisks cannot be included as part of the message.

c.  Ask the user if he wants to encode or decode the message.

d.  To encode a message, replace each character with the tenth character following it in the code array. Any character in the message that doesn't appear in the code array (such as ;) should be left unchanged. Characters appearing as the last ten elements in the code array should be replaced by the first ten elements in the array. Example:

| | |
|---|---|
| The message | 9:25 AM |
| is entered | 9, :,2,5," ",A,M,* |
| and encoded | G:.CHKW |

Decoding works the same way, but replaces each character by the tenth character *preceding* it in the array.

e.  Print the encoded or decoded message.

f.  Ask the program's user whether he has another message to encode or decode. If he has, return to step *b*. If not, terminate. Note that if he has a message longer than thirty characters, he can enter it in segments.

## FOOTNOTES AND REFERENCES

1  See Gear, section 2.5.5, "Character Data," for a discussion of the representation of alphabetic characters inside the computer.

2  Some small computer systems require that each individual string be dimensioned. These systems lack the *string array* capability as such (that is, they allow an array of characters but not an array of strings).

3  The character sequence shown in the table is a subset of the American National Standards Institute (ANSI) character set. Some systems may use a different character set and, therefore, have a different character sequence.

The BASIC programming language was designed originally to handle simple numerical problems and was intended to be only a first step toward more complicated languages such as FORTRAN.

In the intervening years, however, software developers eager to offer potential customers more capabilities than the competition, time-sharing computer manufacturers developing equipment with massive data banks and core storage to lure big business into online processing, university computer-center users becoming increasingly sophisticated—all have combined to extend BASIC (and most other languages) into regions far beyond the intentions of its originators.

The extensions to BASIC that are unique to a handful of developers have not been included in this book. Advances that have been universally accepted and incorporated (such as the capability of manipulating nonnumeric characters) are, of course, discussed. This chapter describes three additional advanced features that have widespread, if not universal, acceptance:

- Multiple assignments
- The ON—GOTO statement (calculated GOTO)
- Logical operators

## MULTIPLE ASSIGNMENTS

Most BASIC systems now permit multiple assignments in one statement.

$$10 \ \text{LET} \ A = B2 = C = D+1$$

After this statement has been executed, the locations labeled A, B2, and C will all contain the value of the expression $(D + 1)$. Do not try to assign a value to an expression. LET $A = A + 1 = C{\uparrow}2$ is an invalid statement. (This error was discussed in our description of the standard LET statement. See chapter 4.)

Chapter

# 11

# Advanced
# Features

### THE CALCULATED GOTO (ON—GOTO)

The combination statement ON—GOTO is, in effect, a conditional branch. It allows you to calculate a value that in turn determines which of several branches to take.
The format is

ON expression GOTO branch-1,b-2,b-3,b-4, . . .

The branches are statement numbers in your program. If the expression has the value 1, then the statement indicated by branch-1 is the next instruction executed. If the value is 2, branch-2 is taken, and so on.
Example :

```
10 ON A/3 GOTO 40, 80, 120, 160, 200
```

If the value of A is 3 (A/3 = 1), statement 40 is executed next. If the value of A is 15 (A/3 = 5), statement 200 is executed next. Only the integer part of the expression is used in determining which branch to take. If A = 11 in the above example, branch-3 is taken (statement 120 is executed next). If you want the calculation to be rounded, add .5 to the expression. (Recall what was said in chapter 7 about rounding by using INT.)
Example :

```
10 ON A/3 + .5 GOTO 40, 80, 120, 160, 200
```

Now if A = 11, branch-4 is taken (A/3 + .5 = 4.167). You can include as many statement numbers as you want to, within the limit of the input line. If the expression's value is less than one or greater than the number of statement numbers provided, BASIC prints an error message.

You may want to provide your own error routines for certain values of an expression. For example, assume you have eight calculations that you usually perform on a set of data. You have written a BASIC program, CALC, to perform five of the eight calculations (numbers 1—4 and 8). When the program is loaded, you must enter the number of the calculation you want to have performed. When this calculation is completed, you can request another. When you have finished, you enter a 9 to cause the program to terminate.

```
10 PRINT "WHICH CALCULATION? ENTER 9 IF DONE"
20 INPUT X
30 IF X<1 THEN 60
40 IF X>9 THEN 60
50 ON X GOTO 100, 200, 300, 400, 80, 80, 80, 500, 600
60 PRINT "INVALID REPLY"
70 GOTO 10
80 PRINT "MANUAL CALCULATION REQUIRED"
90 GOTO 10
100 REM CALCULATION ONE
```

```
     •
     •
     •
19Ø  GOTO 1Ø
2ØØ  REM CALCULATION TWO
     •
     •
29Ø  GOTO 1Ø
3ØØ  REM CALCULATION THREE
     •
     •
39Ø  GOTO 1Ø
4ØØ  REM CALCULATION FOUR
     •
     •
49Ø  GOTO 1Ø
5ØØ  REM CALCULATION EIGHT
     •
     •
59Ø  GOTO 1Ø
6ØØ  END
```

## LOGICAL EXPRESSIONS AND OPERATORS

Logical operations are not used in most BASIC systems. They have been
carried over from FORTRAN to some BASIC systems, but as yet no common
format has been agreed upon.[1]

There are five logical operators: AND, OR, EQV (equivalence), IMP
(implication), and NOT. They are used in conjunction with relational expressions
and logical variables to form logical expressions. As with relational expressions,
logical expressions are either *true* or *false*. Table 2 shows how the truth of a

TABLE 2    Logical Expressions and Operators

| | | |
|---|---|---|
| If expression | A is T T F F | |
| and expression | B is T F T F | |
| A AND | B is T F F F | |
| A OR | B is T T T F | |
| A EQV | B is T F F T | |
| A IMP | B is T F T T | |
| NOT | A   If A is true, | |
| | then NOT A is false. | |
| | If A is false, | |
| | then NOT A is true. | |

logical expression is determined for each of the logical operators. A and B represent relational expressions or logical variables; T stands for *true* and F stands for *false*. For example, if both A and B are true in the logical expression A AND B, the expression is true.

Examples:

`1Ø IF X = 3 OR X = -3 THEN 2ØØ` If either of the relational expressions is true, statement 200 is executed next.

`2Ø IF A<2 AND B<5 THEN 25Ø` If both relational expressions are true, statement 250 is executed next.

Thus a local draft board could write a program that includes statements such as the following where A = age; L = draft-lottery number.

```
5Ø IF A = 19 AND L <= 15Ø THEN 2ØØ
•
•
•
2ØØ PRINT "GREETINGS"
```

A logical variable is considered to be false if its value is zero and true if it is positive or negative.

X = 7   X is true.
Y = Ø   Y is false.
Z = −3   Z is true.

Note that in logical expressions more than one relational operator can be present. You may be able to enter one logical expression in place of several relational expressions. For example:

```
3Ø IF A >= Ø AND A <= 99 OR A >= 2ØØ AND A <= 299 THEN 8Ø
4Ø REM A IS NOT Ø-99 OR 2ØØ-299
•
•
•
8Ø REM A IS IN THE RANGE Ø-99 OR 2ØØ-299
•
•
•
```

The following statements perform the same function without the use of logical operators.

```
30 IF A<0 THEN 40
32 IF A<=99 THEN 80
34 IF A<200 THEN 40
36 IF A<=299 THEN 80
40 REM A IS NOT 0-99 OR 200-299
 •
 •
 •
80 REM A IS IN THE RANGE 0-99 OR 200-299
 •
 •
 •
```

The order of precedence for expressions that include logical operators is as follows:

Functions and arithmetic operations are performed first, in the sequence described in chapter 4.
Relational operations are tested next.
Logical operations are tested last, usually in this sequence:
> NOT
> AND
> OR
> IMP
> EQV

Thus in the example

```
100 IF Q>X AND Q < X*3 OR X=0 THEN 190
```

(assuming $Q=10$ and $X=5$), BASIC performs the arithmetic operations first.

$X*3 = 15$
Then it tests the relational operations.
$Q>X$ is true
$Q<X*3$ is true
$X=0$ is false

The logical operations are tested last, AND before OR.

IF Q>X and Q<X*3 OR X=Ø THEN 19Ø

IF true AND true OR false THEN 19Ø

IF     true     OR false THEN 19Ø

IF              true       THEN 19Ø

Statement 190 is executed next.

In complicated logical expressions, use parentheses to avoid ambiguity. The following statement selects men and women to be considered for a job that has age and height restrictions.

```
60 IF (S$="F" AND A<=21 AND H>=65 OR (S$="M" AND A>=25 AND H>=7Ø) THEN 90
```

The order of precedence just shown may differ from system to system. Before attempting logical operations you must find out:

- Whether your BASIC compiler accepts such operations
- If so, how logical variables are defined in your system
- What the rules of precedence governing logical operators for your particular system are.


### EXERCISES

1. Write a program to see whether your system allows you to assign a value to more than one variable in a single LET statement.
   a. Assign the value 15 to A
   b. In one statement, assign the value of A/3 + 1 to X, Y, and Z
   c. Print the values of A, X, Y, and Z
   If you get a syntax error message, reenter step *b* as three LET statements and try again.

2. Use ON—GOTO statements in a program that calculates the number of workdays (Monday—Friday) in a given month. Let the program's user enter the month (1—12) and the starting day of the month (1—7, where 1 stands for Sunday). Be sure to test the user's input for validity before you continue the calculation. If he enters month 2 (February), ask him if this is leap year.
   There are two basic approaches you can take to this problem.
   *A*. You can devise some plan (algorithm) for *calculating* the answer. This approach will probably result in a program with relatively more complicated calculations and fewer statements.
   *B*. You can start with the facts that every month has:
   - At least 4 weeks, or 20 work days
   - Plus 0, 1, 2, or 3 more work days, depending on the number of days in the month and the starting day of the month.
   You can then solve your programming problem by logical tests and branch-

ing. This approach will probably result in a somewhat longer program with very simple calculations. (One possible solution is given in appendix B.)

As a programmer you will often face a choice between a less sophisticated, longer solution and a more sophisticated shorter one. Some programmers will always choose the most sophisticated and shortest solution, no matter how long it takes to design and debug the program. Good programmers look for a practical medium.

3.  Test to see whether logical operations work on your system; enter the program:

```
1Ø IF 2+2 = 4 AND 4+4 = 8 THEN 4Ø
2Ø PRINT "FALSE"
3Ø STOP
4Ø PRINT "TRUE"
5Ø END
```

This program is intended solely to test the capabilities of your BASIC compiler. You don't need a computer to tell you that $2+2 = 4$.

4.  If you didn't get a syntax error when you tried exercise 3, write programs to see whether your system accepts OR, EQV, IMP, and NOT. Try combinations of tests to see whether the order of precedence is as shown under *Logical Expressions and Operators*, page 105, in this chapter. Use parentheses to override the rules of precedence.

Examples:      $-1Ø>Ø$ OR $-3<Ø$ AND $2+2=4$ should be true
               $-3<Ø$ OR $-1Ø>Ø$ AND $2+2=4$ should be false
               $(-3<Ø$ OR $-1Ø>Ø)$ AND $2+2=4$ should be true

Use numerical constants and simple tests.

If some of the logical operations aren't available on your system, don't worry. You may need a few more statements, but you can always perform logical tests without them. And don't worry if you don't fully understand equivalence and implication. They're used mainly by logicians.

## FOOTNOTES AND REFERENCES

1    Gear, section 2.5.6, "Logical Data."

BASIC program errors fall into two general classifications: logic errors (errors in program design) and syntax errors (violations of the rules of the BASIC programming language).

The latter might be caused by misspelling or mistyping a keyword (for example, GOSIB instead of GOSUB), by omitting a parenthesis or quotation mark, or a similar error. Most syntax errors are recognized by the BASIC compiler and are flagged by diagnostic messages such as:

ERROR LINE 33Ø
"DEF" STATEMENT USES FUNCTION NAME NOT STARTING WITH "FN"
or simply
ILLEGAL INSTRUCTION IN 33Ø

The purpose of this chapter is to help you clear up those logic errors that elude the compiler but nevertheless prevent your program from accomplishing its purpose. The best way to clear up errors is, of course, to keep them out of your program in the first place. Take the word *"pre*-caution" literally.

## PROGRAM DESIGN

Before designing your program, you should imbue your mind with as many clichés of the following type as possible:

HASTE MAKES WASTE.
A COMPUTER IS NO SUBSTITUTE FOR THINKING.
AN OUNCE OF PREVENTION IS WORTH A POUND OF CURE.
A STITCH IN TIME . . .

Having proceeded past this first stage of enlightenment, you should keep the following suggestions in mind.[1]

- Make liberal use of REM statements throughout your program.
- Variables should be as mnemonic as possible (for example, T for Total, I for Interest, R2 for Square Root, N$ for Name).
- If the program is large, develop it in modules or segments. Break it into

Chapter

# 12

# Debugging Aids

subroutines using GOSUB, or think of decision points or loops (FOR–NEXT) as forming independent blocks. This approach makes the next stage of error prevention easier.

## TESTING YOUR PROGRAM

As in thoughtful program design, judicious testing can catch many errors in the earliest stages of program development. One way to test your program or program segments is to pretend that you are the computer. This is a form of *desk checking*. Go through the program step by step, using data yielding results that can be verified easily. Try this on NAMSRT in chapter 10 or RAIN3 in chapter 9.

After desk checking, or if your program is too complex for desk checking, take full advantage of your interactive terminal. As mentioned in chapter 2, the rapid response available in interactive programming gives you a tremendous advantage over the programmer who uses traditional batch-processing methods. You can enter your program on the terminal a segment at a time, test that portion thoroughly, and then enter the next segment.

The key word in the last paragraph is *thoroughly*. The main consideration in testing is to make sure your hypothetical data tests every possible situation, that every possible branch is taken, and every calculation is performed.

Again, data should be simple enough so that calculations can be verified easily or samples that return known results should be used. In some cases, such as the solution of equations, a calculation can be tested by feeding results back into the problem. For example, using this method, we could have tested the performance of the simultaneous linear-equation program, LINEAR, page 93, chapter 9.

```
10 READ X1, X2, X3
20 LET Z(1) = 3*X1 + X2 - 2*X3
30 LET Z(2) = -2*X1 + 2*X2 + 5*X3
40 LET Z(3) = 4*X2 + X3
50 PRINT Z(1); Z(2); Z(3)
60 DATA 3, 7, -2
70 END
RUNNH


20    -2    26

DONE
```

The results of this program are the same as the values appearing on the right side of the equal sign in the three original equations.

## TRACING

In more complicated debugging situations we may want to know the intermediate results at crucial checkpoints in our program. Thus, instead of knowing only that we've made a mistake *somewhere* in a lengthy process, we'll be able to pinpoint the bug to a specific series of steps.

Such intermediate checking is called a *program trace*. In BASIC, this operation is performed by imbedding PRINT statements at our checkpoints—for example, inside a FOR—NEXT loop or just before an IF—THEN decision point. These PRINT statements can be removed from the final version of the program.

Example :

```
850 INPUT A,B
855 PRINT "A AND B ENTERED"
860 IF A<0 THEN 1000
870 FOR C = 2 TO B STEP 2
880 LET A = A+C
885 PRINT C;A
890 NEXT C
895 PRINT "B WAS" B "LAST A WAS" A
900 GOTO 850
    .
    .
    .
```

The statements numbered 855, 885, and 895 could all be removed once we determine that this program segment is performing properly. If the simulation, desk checking, terminal testing, and tracing methods should all fail to uncover your error, you would be wise to request a listing of your program and then give the terminal a rest while you revert to ground zero.

HASTE MAKES WASTE.

A COMPUTER IS NO SUBSTITUTE FOR THINKING.

AN OUNCE OF PREVENTION . . .


### FOOTNOTES AND REFERENCES

1   Gear, section 4.4, includes a list of the most common sources of program errors.

APPENDIX

# A

# SUMMARY of
# BASIC FEATURES

BASIC statements, functions, and operators are grouped in the following tables for quick reference. In the syntax lists, brackets enclose optional parameters—for example, [num]. All other punctuation is part of the statement syntax. Chapter references are included, should you want to review a particular statement.

## LEGEND

num   A numerical constant, in integer, decimal, or exponential form
exp   A mathematical expression—can be simply a numerical variable or numerical constant
var   A numerical variable name
var$   A string variable name

TABLE 1  BASIC Statement Syntax

| Statement | Meaning | Chapter |
|---|---|---|
| DATA num [, num . . . , num]<br><br>DATA "string" [, "string" . . . , "string"] | Supplies data for READ statement.<br>Numerical and string forms can be combined. | 5<br><br>10 |
| DEF FNa = exp | Defines a function named FNa, where "a" is any letter. | 7 |
| DIM var(exp[,exp])<br>DIM var$(exp) | Used to dimension numerical or string arrays containing a subscript greater than 10. | 9<br>10 |
| END | Highest-numbered statement in program; halts compilation. | 6 |
| FOR var = exp TO exp [STEP exp]<br>.<br>.<br>.<br>NEXT var | Loop control statements; "var" must be identical in both statements. | 6 |
| GOSUB statement n<br>.<br>.<br>.<br>statement n<br>.<br>.<br>.<br>RETURN | Transfers control to the subroutine beginning at statement n and then returns control to the statement following GOSUB. | 8 |
| GOTO statement n | Branches to statement n. | 6 |
| IF relational exp THEN statement n | If the relational expression is true, branches to statement n | 6<br>10 |
| INPUT var [, var . . . , var]<br>INPUT var$ [, var$ . . . , var$] | Requests numerical or alphamerical data at program execution time. Forms can be combined. | 5 |
| LET var = exp<br>LET var$ = "string" | Assigns value of expression or string to variable. | 4<br>10 |

TABLE 1   BASIC Statement Syntax (*cont'd.*)

| Statement | Meaning | Chapter |
|---|---|---|
| LET var = var [= var . . . = var] = exp | Multiple assignment. | 11 |
| PRINT | Skips one line. | 5 |
| PRINT var<br>PRINT var$<br>PRINT "string"<br>PRINT exp | Types out variable or literal values. Forms can be combined. | 5 |
| READ var [, var . . . , var]<br>READ var$ [, var$ . . . , var$] | Reads numerical or alphamerical values from DATA statements. Forms can be combined. | 5 |
| REM anything | Comment statement. | 3<br>12 |
| RESTORE | Resets READ pointer to beginning of first DATA statement. | 5<br>10 |
| RETURN | See GOSUB above. | |
| STOP | Program terminator: branches to END statement. | 6 |

TABLE 2   Matrix Statements
(Chapter 9)

| Format | Meaning |
|---|---|
| MAT INPUT var [, var . . . , var] | Reads data into previously dimensioned matrices at execution time. |
| MAT PRINT var [, var . . . , var] | Types designated matrices. |
| MAT READ var [, var . . . , var] | Reads data into previously dimensioned matrices. |
| MAT y = x | Sets matrix y equivalent to matrix x. |
| MAT z = x + y | Adds the elements of matrix x to the corresponding elements of matrix y; stores the results in matrix z. |
| MAT z = x − y | Subtracts matrix y from matrix x; stores result in matrix z. |
| MAT z = x*y | Multiplies matrix x by matrix y; product stored in z. |
| MAT z = (exp)*x | Elements of matrix x are multiplied by the expression; product stored in z. |
| MAT z = INV(x) | Inverts matrix x; new version stored in matrix z. |
| MAT z = TRN(x) | Transposes matrix x; new version stored in matrix z. |
| MAT x = ZER | Fills matrix x with zeros. |
| MAT x = CON | Fills matrix x with ones. |
| MAT x = IDN | Matrix x is set up as an identity matrix. |

TABLE 3   Precedence of Operators

| Operator | Meaning | Chapter |
|---|---|---|
| +, − (unary) | Unary plus or minus | 4 |
| ↑ | Exponentiation | 4 |
| *, / | Multiplication and division | 4 |
| +, − | Addition and subtraction | 4 |
| =, <, < =, > =. >, < > | Relational operators | 6 |
| NOT* | Boolean NOT | 11 |
| AND* | Boolean AND | 11 |
| OR* | Boolean OR | 11 |
| IMP* | Implication | 11 |
| EQV* | Equivalence | 11 |

*Advanced feature

TABLE 4. BASIC Functions

| Format | Meaning | Chapter |
|--------|---------|---------|
| ABS(x) | Returns absolute value of x | 7 |
| ATN(x)* | Returns arctangent of x | 7 |
| COS(x)** | Returns cosine of x | 7 |
| EXP(x) | Returns natural exponent of x | 7 |
| INT(x) | Returns integer part of x | 7 |
| LOG(x) | Returns natural logarithm of x | 7 |
| RND[(x)] | Random number generator | 7 |
| SGN | Returns sign of x | 7 |
| SIN(x)** | Returns sine of x | 7 |
| SQR(x) | Returns square root of x | 3,7 |
| TAB(x) | Tabs printout to print position x | 5,7 |
| TAN(x)** | Returns tangent of x | 7 |

*Answer is in radians
**x = angle in radians

# Solutions to Selected Exercises

Following are sample solutions to some of the exercises. Remember there is no one correct solution to a programming problem. Your solution may differ significantly.

**Chapter 4, exercise 4, page 35**

```
1Ø LET L = 1.72
2Ø LET W = 2.91
3Ø LET A = L*W
4Ø LET C = 2*L + 2*W
5Ø PRINT "AREA IS" A
6Ø PRINT "CIRCUMFERENCE IS" C
7Ø END
RUNNH


AREA IS 5.ØØ52
CIRCUMFERENCE IS 9.26

DONE
```

**Chapter 6, exercise 6, page 56**

```
1Ø REM E = NUMBER ERRORS, X = MULTIPLICAND, Y = MULTIPLIER,
15  REM                                  A = STUDENT'S ANSWER
2Ø LET E = Ø
3Ø FOR X = 2 TO 12
4Ø FOR Y = 2 TO 12
5Ø PRINT X "X" Y "?";
6Ø INPUT A
7Ø IF A = X*Y THEN 1ØØ
8Ø LET E = E+1
9Ø PRINT X "X" Y "=" X*Y
1ØØ NEXT Y
11Ø NEXT X
12Ø IF E > 5 THEN 2Ø
13Ø IF E < 3 THEN 16Ø
14Ø PRINT "GOOD"
15Ø STOP
16Ø PRINT "VERY GOOD"
17Ø END
RUNNH


2     X 2     ?4
2     X 3     ?6
2     X 4     ?9
2     X 4     = 8
2     X 5     ?10
2     X 6     ?12
2     X 7     ?13
2     X 7     = 14
2     X 8     ?16
2     X 9     ?18
```

| 2 | X 10 | ?20 |
|---|------|-----|
| 2 | X 11 | ?22 |
| 2 | X 12 | ?24 |
| 3 | X 2  | ?6  |
| 3 | X 3  | ?9  |
| 3 | X 4  | ?12 |
| 3 | X 5  | ?15 |
| 3 | X 6  | ?18 |
| 3 | X 7  | ?20 |
| 3 | X 7  | = 21 |
| 3 | X 8  | ?24 |
| 3 | X 9  | ?27 |
| 3 | X 10 | ?30 |
| 3 | X 11 | ?33 |
| 3 | X 12 | ?36 |
| 4 | X 2  | ?8  |
| 4 | X 3  | ?12 |
| 4 | X 4  | ?16 |
| 4 | X 5  | ?20 |
| 4 | X 6  | ?24 |
| 4 | X 7  | ?28 |

etc.

## Chapter 7, exercise 3, page 64

```
10 LET X = 9
20 LET X = X + .1
30 IF X↑2 < 93 THEN 20
40 LET X = X - .1
50 LET X = X + .01
60 IF X↑2 < 93 THEN 50
70 LET X = X - .01
80 LET X = X + .001
90 IF X↑2 < 93 THEN 80
100 LET X = X - .001
110 LET X = X + .0001
120 IF X↑2 < 93 THEN 110
130 LET X = X - .0001
140 LET R = INT(X*10↑3 + .5)/10↑3
150 PRINT "CALCULATED SQUARE ROOT IS" R
160 PRINT "SQR(93)"  SQR(93)
170 END
RUNNH


CALCULATED SQUARE ROOT IS 9.644
SQR(93) 9.64365

DONE
```

**Chapter 9, exercise 4, page 95**

```
1    DIM G[6,6],R[6,6]
1Ø   REM G(I,J) = THE NUMBER OF TIMES I BEAT J
2Ø   REM R(I,J) = THE TOTAL NUMBER OF RUNS I SCORED OVER J
3Ø   MAT G=ZER
4Ø   MAT R=ZER
5Ø   READ T1,S1,T2,S2
6Ø   IF T1=9 THEN 16Ø
7Ø   IF S1 <> S2 THEN 1ØØ
8Ø   PRINT "TIE: REENTER AFTER REPLAY"
9Ø   GOTO 5Ø
1ØØ  IF S1<S2 THEN 13Ø
11Ø  LET G[T1,T2]=G[T1,T2]+1
12Ø  GOTO 14Ø
13Ø  LET G[T2,T1]=G[T2,T1]+1
14Ø  LET R[T1,T2]=R[T1,T2]+S1
15Ø  LET R[T2,T1]=R[T2,T1]+S2
155  GOTO 5Ø
16Ø  PRINT "TEAM","WINS","LOSSES","AVE NO. RUNS"
17Ø  FOR X=1 TO 6
18Ø  REM W = WINS, L = LOSSES, N = TOTAL RUNS
19Ø  LET W=L=N=Ø
2ØØ  FOR Y=1 TO 6
21Ø  LET W=W+G[X,Y]
22Ø  LET L=L+G[Y,X]
23Ø  LET N=N+R[X,Y]
24Ø  NEXT Y
25Ø  PRINT X,W,L,N/(W+L)
26Ø  NEXT X
27Ø  PRINT "ENTER TEAM NUMBERS: ENTER 9,9 IF DONE"
28Ø  INPUT A,B
29Ø  IF A=9 THEN 52Ø
3ØØ  PRINT "TEAM"A"BEAT"B; G[A,B]"TIMES"
305  PRINT "TEAM"B"BEAT"A; G[B,A]"TIMES"
31Ø  PRINT "TEAM"A"AVE RUNS"R[A,B]/(G[A,B]+G[B,A])
32Ø  PRINT "TEAM"B"AVE RUNS"R[B,A]/(G[B,A]+G[A,B])
325  GOTO 27Ø
33Ø  DATA 1,5,3,2
34Ø  DATA 2,4,1,1
35Ø  DATA 1,3,2,7
36Ø  DATA 2,Ø,4,1
```

```
370     DATA 2,0,6,1
380     DATA 3,1,5,3
390     DATA 1,4,3,2
400     DATA 4,2,1,7
410     DATA 3,11,2,1
420     DATA 4,6,6,2
430     DATA 2,1,5,2
440     DATA 5,3,4,4
450     DATA 2,2,5,1
460     DATA 3,3,4,2
470     DATA 6,0,3,2
480     DATA 6,2,2,0
490     DATA 5,1,1,4
500     DATA 3,9,6,2
510     DATA 9,9,9,9
520     END
RUNNH
```

| TEAM | WINS | LOSSES | AVE NO. RUNS |
|------|------|--------|--------------|
| 1 | 4 | 2 | 4 |
| 2 | 3 | 5 | 1.875 |
| 3 | 4 | 3 | 4.28571 |
| 4 | 3 | 2 | 3 |
| 5 | 2 | 3 | 2 |
| 6 | 2 | 3 | 1.4 |

```
ENTER TEAM NUMBERS: ENTER 9,9 IF DONE
?1,2
TEAM 1    BEAT 2      0    TIMES
TEAM 2    BEAT 1      2    TIMES
TEAM 1    AVE RUNS 2
TEAM 2    AVE RUNS 5.5
ENTER TEAM NUMBERS: ENTER 9,9 IF DONE
?2,5
TEAM 2    BEAT 5      1    TIMES
TEAM 5    BEAT 2      1    TIMES
TEAM 2    AVE RUNS 1.5
TEAM 5    AVE RUNS 1.5
ENTER TEAM NUMBERS: ENTER 9,9 IF DONE
?9,9

DONE
```

Chapter 11, exercise 2, page 108

```
1Ø    PRINT "ENTER MONTH 1-12 OR 99 IF DONE"
15    INPUT M
2Ø    IF M=99 ,THEN 27Ø
3Ø    IF M<1 THEN 1Ø
4Ø    IF M>12 THEN 1Ø
45    PRINT "ENTER DAY 1-7 (SUN = 1)"
5Ø    INPUT D
55    IF D<1 THEN 45
6Ø    IF D>7 THEN 45
7Ø    ON M GOTO 9Ø,13Ø,9Ø,11Ø,9Ø,11Ø,9Ø,9Ø,11Ø,9Ø,11Ø,9Ø
8Ø    REM 31 DAYS IN MONTH
9Ø    ON D GOTO 23Ø,25Ø,25Ø,25Ø,23Ø,21Ø,21Ø
1ØØ   REM 3Ø DAYS IN MONTH
11Ø   ON D GOTO 21Ø,23Ø,23Ø,23Ø,23Ø,21Ø,19Ø
12Ø   REM FEB
13Ø   PRINT "LEAP YEAR? Y OR N"
14Ø   INPUT R$
15Ø   IF R$="N" THEN 19Ø
16Ø   IF R$="Y" THEN 18Ø
17Ø   GOTO 13Ø
18Ø   ON D GOTO 19Ø,21Ø,21Ø,21Ø,21Ø,21Ø,19Ø
19Ø   PRINT "2Ø WORK DAYS"
2ØØ   GOTO 1Ø
21Ø   PRINT "21 WORK DAYS"
22Ø   GOTO 1Ø
23Ø   PRINT "22 WORK DAYS"
24Ø   GOTO 1Ø
25Ø   PRINT "23 WORK DAYS"
26Ø   GOTO 1Ø
27Ø   END
RUNNH


ENTER MONTH 1-12 OR 99 IF DONE
?1
ENTER DAY 1-7 (SUN = 1)
?2
23 WORK DAYS
ENTER MONTH 1-12 OR 99 IF DONE
?2
ENTER DAY 1-7 (SUN = 1)
?5
LEAP YEAR? Y OR N
?N
2Ø WORK DAYS
ENTER MONTH 1-12 OR 99 IF DONE
?3
```

```
ENTER DAY 1-7 (SUN = 1)
?5
22 WORK DAYS
ENTER MONTH 1-12 OR 99 IF DONE
?4
ENTER DAY 1-7 (SUN = 1)
?1
21 WORK DAYS
ENTER MONTH 1-12 OR 99 IF DONE
?5
ENTER DAY 1-7 (SUN = 1)
?3
23 WORK DAYS
ENTER MONTH 1-12 OR 99 IF DONE
?6
ENTER DAY 1-7 (SUN = 1)
?6
21 WORK DAYS
ENTER MONTH 1-12 OR 99 IF DONE
?7
ENTER DAY 1-7 (SUN = 1)
?1
22 WORK DAYS
ENTER MONTH 1-12 OR 99 IF DONE
?8
ENTER DAY 1-7 (SUN = 1)
?4
23 WORK DAYS
ENTER MONTH 1-12 OR 99 IF DONE
?99

DONE
```

*Address*   A number designating a specific location in the memory of a computer.

*Alphanumerics*   Alphabetic or numerical characters, usually combined.

*Argument*   The variable operand or modifier of a program command.

*Assembler*   A program that translates assembly-language source programs into object code understandable to the computer. *See* Object Program.

*Central Processing Unit*   The part of a computer that performs the computational operations requested by a user at his terminal. Referred to as the CPU.

*Character Set*   A set of symbols consisting of the letters A to Z, the digits 0 to 9, and selected punctuation marks and mathematical symbols.

*Compiler*   A program that translates high-level source-language statements into object code understandable to the computer. *See* Object Program.

*Console*   A terminal containing key, button, switch, or dial controls used in communicating with the computer. *See* Teletypewriter.

*Constant*   Information whose value or meaning is fixed. *See* Variable Name.

*Debug*   To detect and remove program mistakes.

*Default Value*   An assumed value in the absence of a specific indication of what the value should be. Usually applied to variables in the argument portion of a command statement.

*Execution*   The interpretation by the CPU of a machine instruction, and performance of the indicated operation(s) on the specified data.

*Executive Language*   The software system that handles input/output, editing, and similar functions for subsystems such as FORTRAN and BASIC.

*File*   A named collection of related information (for example, program instructions or input data). A file may be temporary or permanent (saved).

*Hardware*   The magnetic, mechanical, electrical, and electronic devices, or components of a computer system. *See* System Software.

*Initialize*   To set various counters, switches, and addresses to zero or other starting values at prescribed points in a program.

*Input*   Information transferred from an external medium into the internal storage of a computer. In some cases (as in the BASIC DATA statement), input can be part of a program.

*Listing*   A printed reproduction of program statements arranged in sequential order.

*Logging On/Off*   The procedures for linking a terminal to a computer, and for unlinking from the computer when finished.

# A BASIC Glossary

*Loop*   A sequence of instructions that is repeated until a terminating condition is reached.

*Memory*   The internal-hardware area used to store information needed by the central processor. It is also referred to as primary storage or core storage.

*Object Program*   A sequence of instructions, directly comprehensible to the computer, to perform a set of arithmetic and logic operations.

*Output*   Information transferred from the internal storage of a computer to any one of several external media (for example, paper, punched paper tape, or drum or disc storage).

*Source Program*   The program statements prepared by the user and later translated into machine language by a compiler or assembler.

*Statement*   A single program step consisting of a keyword (such as GOTO) and its arguments.

*Syntax*   The rules for constructing the sequence of characters that make up program statements, file names, and similar constructs.

*System Software*   Various internal programs that facilitate the programmer's efficient use of the computer hardware (for example, compilers, mathematical routines, utilities).

*Teletypewriter*   A point in an interactive communication network where data can be entered or typed out. It is variously referred to as a terminal, console keyboard, TTY, or by the trade name *Teletype*.

*User Number*   Account-identification characters assigned to customers by a system owner.

*User Password*   A code assigned to a customer to prevent unauthorized use of his account.

*Variable name*   The name assigned to a primary storage location that can assume any of a given set of values. *See* Constant.

# Index

The text was set in 9 point Univers 55
by Holmes Typography Inc. of San Jose, California, and
printed by The George Banta Company of Menasha, Wisconsin.

Project Editor: Toni Marshall
Production Editor: Barbara Carpenter
Sponsoring Editor: Stephen Mitchell
Designer: Michael Rogondino

456/5432